40 DAYS TO SUCCESS IN REAL ESTATE INVESTING

40 DAYS TO SUCCESS IN REAL ESTATE INVESTING

ROBERT SHEMIN

WILEY

John Wiley & Sons, Inc.

Published by John Wiley & Sons, Inc., Hoboken, New Jersey.
Published simultaneously in Canada.

For general information on our other products and services please contact our Customer Care Department within the United States at (800) 762-2974, outside the United States at (317) 572-3993 or fax (317) 572-4002.

Wiley also publishes its books in a variety of electronic formats. Some content that appears in print may not be available in electronic books. For more information about Wiley products, visit our web site at www.Wiley.com.

Library of Congress Cataloging-in-Publication Data:
Shemin, Robert, 1963–
    40 days to success in real estate investing / by Robert Shemin.
        p. cm.
    Includes index.
    ISBN 0-471-69482-7 (pbk. : alk. paper)
    1. Real estate investment.   I. Title: Forty days to success in real estate investing.   II. Title.
HD1382.5.S4677 2005
332.63'24—dc22

                                                                            2004062475

Printed in the United States of America.

10 9 8 7 6 5 4 3 2 1

To Alexander,
may you have more success in all areas
of your life than you can dream of.

Complimentary $150 Value

with the purchase of this book

Go to www.sheminrealestate.com NOW and register for your 40-day Plan for Success daily emails and scheduled teleconference at *no charge*.

Bonus—Receive a free newsletter $40 Value if you register NOW.

Happy investing!

CONTENTS

CONTENTS

Contents

ACKNOWLEDGMENTS

A special thank you to all of the people who have made this book possible: Mike Hamilton and the great team at John Wiley & Sons, Inc.; Barbara McNichol (www.barbaramcnichol.com) a talented editor who has made all of my books a reality and her editorial assistant Sherry Sterling; Andrea Ramos, a fantastic associate and person; Paul Bauer, a wonderful agent and friend; Brian McAdams, Jeff Vihari, Cameron, and Hisha at EMS.

Thanks to Mom and Dad; without them, neither this book nor I would have happened.

Thanks to my fellow investors, speakers, authors, and friends who inspire me—Wright Thurston, Dr. A.C. Loury, David Finkel, Peter Conti, Russ Whitney, Jeffrey Taylor (www.MrLandlord.com), Robert Allen, Lee Phillips, Vena Jones-Coe, Lundy Patton, Duran and Sharon, Jeff Petroko, David Duech, Chris Cooper, and Heather Seitz.

A special hello and thanks to Tamara Davis, Lisa Delman, Rav Chaim from Jerusalem, Anthony Cherry, Luisa Garcia (my trainer), Shakira, Bruce Springsteen, Donald Trump, Robert Kiyosaki, President Jimmy Carter, Dr. Richard Hersch, Dr. Keith South, the Kaballah Center, Garth Brooks, P. Diddy, Ludacris, Lil' Kim, and Bill, Sam, Steve and all of the great people at the Learning Annex (www.learningannex.com).

And thanks to my students and to *you* for reading this book.

Happy investing and learning. Have more fun!

If you want to get started in real estate by focusing on simple activities over a 40-day period, this book is written specifically for you. It's not a question of whether this plan for success will work—if you follow these action plans faithfully, you *will* succeed. How will you know? You'll work to find good deals in real estate, make offers, and start making money.

Start with the mind-set that failure is not an option. There's no going back; once you learn something, you know it. Through my seminars and tapes, I've spoken to a hundred thousand real estate investors, from beginners to pros. No matter what the level of experience, everyone asks me the same questions: What should I do this week? How can I get started? or (for the pros) How can I get focused?

The information in this book will help you get focused, get going, and stop worrying or wondering, "What do I do tomorrow? What do I do next week?"

What Determines Your Success?

Anyone can follow these ideas and become an investor. You don't need experience or a license. You don't even need to be a real estate broker. You just require these three things: desire, time, and commitment.

Desire

Your success in real estate investing is determined by your desire. You must already have desire, or you wouldn't be reading this book. The question is: What do you desire? Pinning that down is the focus of Day 1.

Time

Any business you're in requires you to dedicate time. I recommend devoting between 5 and 10 hours a week working on your real estate business. That's exactly how this 40-Day Plan is designed to work. If you're willing to consistently dedicate at least five hours a week to real estate for the next six weeks, you'll get results.

Commitment

The third requirement is commitment. I think most people fail in any business, but especially in real estate, because they try it for only two weeks with a part-time focus. After a few phone calls, they decide this particular road to riches doesn't work.

When I started in real estate investing, I decided to make a five-year, part-time commitment. I told myself that I would review the situation at the five-year mark and decide whether to continue. Of course, six months later, I felt like quitting, mostly because I didn't have the systems in place that you'll have after reading this book.

Today, I'm glad I didn't quit. At the 12-year mark, I made more money from one deal I did last year than I made for the entire first two years I was in real estate. Just as in running any business, you'll get better as you go.

Realize that you don't have to know everything there is to know about real estate or be supersharp. Nor do you have to have a lot of money or credit to get started. The main thing is simply to stick with it.

A student of mine in San Diego had been dabbling in real estate investing for seven months, but hadn't adopted the action plans I'd laid out. Instead of following this simple plan, she made up her own, trying this and that. After plodding along for almost 30 weeks, she still hadn't found a deal and was frustrated.

I asked her to stick with it a little longer. She followed my system more closely, found a deal through a real estate agent, bought, fixed up, and sold a house and made $80,000! She recently bought a second investment house and will likely make $180,000—that's in her pocket. Do you think she's glad she stuck with these plans?

Dispelling Doubts

Do you wonder whether real estate investing really works or whether you're suited to it? You probably know people who have made a lot of money in real estate—most of them by accident because they bought one house and it doubled in value. Consider this: If these people made money in real estate by accident, just on their own home without even trying, then you have a chance to make some real money in real estate.

I wonder about people who bought a house to live in, made $100,000 in three years on it, and still spend 50 hours a week at a job they don't like. Why don't they spend more time on real estate and less time at jobs they don't like?

Even if you see the potential in real estate investing, you might decide you don't want to be a real estate investor. I have news for you. You are in real estate, whether you want to be or not. You have to live *somewhere*. You're either buying a house for yourself or you're paying rent. So why not at least learn how to make money on your most important investment?

After reading and completing the exercises in this book, you'll know how to buy your own home for at least 20 percent below market value. Twenty percent on a $200,000 house means you'll save $40,000. If you do that every five years, the dollars add up.

If you're renting, consider lease optioning, which is renting with the option to buy. That way, you won't be throwing all your rent dollars away. Right now, if you're renting for $1,000 a month, what do you have to show for it at the end of the year? Twelve cancelled checks. You've received no tax break, no ownership interest, and little benefit in return for your hard-earned money. You can change that.

If so many people make money in real estate by accident, how much can you make if you do it on purpose? In today's market, people ask me if there's a real estate bubble—and a time when that bubble could burst. Some like to talk themselves out of doing real estate investing. They say real estate is too risky. Prices are too high. They shouldn't get in. Often, they suffer from paralysis of analysis. But consider this: Because you can make money in real estate without committing your own money, there is almost no market risk. For example, I do wholesaling, which means I find property for a good price, put it under contract, and sell it before I have to close on the sale. I don't care whether the market is going up or down next quarter. In wholesaling, I'm in and out before the next quarter comes.

If you rehab houses, you can buy, fix up, and sell a house in about six months. With this approach, you're not concerned about what the market will do in two or three years. If you do lease options (that is, rent with the option to buy), you lock in your purchase price when you make the deal. If the market goes up, you have an opportunity to sell and make a lot of money. If, on the other hand, the market goes down, you are not obligated to exercise your option to buy the property. You just leave after the lease is up and reduce your market risk to zero.

Risk Factors

Rather than assess what your risk is for getting into real estate, assess what your risk is for *not* getting into real estate. That's the real question. What has your risk been for the last several years if you *haven't* been buying real estate? A lot. Most likely, real estate values will continue to rise. If you stay in certain markets for the long run, you'll probably always do okay. If you're in the stock market or real estate market and buy good deals every month, you won't care if the market goes down next year. Next year, you're still buying, so you're benefiting from those less expensive prices.

Compare real estate to the stock market. Stockholders who panic when the market goes down might sell all their stocks. By doing that, they lock in their losses. If they had held on to those stocks for five to ten years, the value of their investment probably would have returned to a higher level. Similarly, with real estate, if investors can hang in long enough, time will fix almost any problem.

> Many years ago, I bought some duplexes in not such a good part of Nashville. It turned out to be a bad deal because I paid too much money for them. I paid the full market value of what they were worth at the time. These duplexes needed more repair work than I'd realized, though, and not surprisingly, the first year or two I owned them, I didn't make any money because of expensive repairs. Then, the neighborhood got better, people started fixing up their properties, and my bad deal almost tripled in value. Time fixed this mistake and can fix almost any mistake you make.

If you have short-term goals, get in and out of the market using wholesaling, lease optioning, and rehabbing. With these approaches, you don't have to worry about what the market will do years from now.

If you're holding properties for the long term and do it properly, by following this 40-Day Plan, you won't have much market risk because you're always buying, you're always able to hang on, and time will fix almost any problem.

Why Real Estate Investing?

As a real estate investor, you have your own business—a business that can make a handsome profit. When you're in business, you're always buying and selling something. Your profit depends on the volume of sales or the cost of each item. For example, as a waiter in a restaurant, I used to get a tip based on the price of the customer's dinner. After working at a $10-a-dinner establishment where my average tip was $1.50, I got smart and worked at a better restaurant in which most dinners cost $40, raising my average tip to $6.

I increased my earnings almost five-fold, and I was still taking one plate of food to the table. It's just that the food was more expensive. I was doing the same amount of work, but making more money. In a similar way, you can work smarter, not harder, in real estate, raking in more money by doing deals with high-ticket items.

Real estate investing has several advantages over other businesses.

Appreciation

Appreciation rates are generally 3 percent to 6 percent a year, which means approximately every 10 years, a property doubles in value. When is the time to get into real estate? Today!

Tax Advantages

Wealthy people focus on one basic thing—after-tax dollars. This book provides information about some general tax considerations as you get started in real estate investing.

If you work for a company or corporation, you probably don't get any work-related tax write-offs; they go to your employer. Your exemptions would be your children, charitable donations, and mortgage interest on your home, which is your largest tax deduction. But if you own your own business, you'll realize a number of tax advantages. (Consult with your accountant about various tax laws that apply to you.) You can write off almost any expenses related to your business. As the owner of a real estate business, you can also write off depreciation and mortgage interest. Other tax benefits include using a 1031 tax-free exchange, self-directed IRA, or pension plan to buy and sell real estate, making it possible to pay no taxes or to defer taxes on your gains.

What's more, as a business owner, you can start a self-employed pension plan, writing off up to $40,000 (according to a sliding scale) of your first year's earnings right off the top. Go to my web site at www.sheminrealestate.com to link with companies that can get you started with a retirement plan. I am not affiliated with these companies, nor do I profit from them—I just think they are good resources for you, as they have been for me.

Debt or Leverage

You'll likely borrow funds to buy real estate. The idea is not to buy real estate without *any* money; it's to buy real estate without using *your* personal funds. What other businesses can you start and have funded by other people? Very few.

Rent Covers Expenses

Your costs to maintain the property are generally covered by rents you collect for properties you hold over time.

Supply and Demand

When you own property, you have the supply, and your property will be in demand. Of course, you have to analyze the market to understand how the supply and demand principle works in your locality.

When I first got into real estate, I thought there was only one way to make money: Borrow money to buy a property, fix it up, and rent it out. Tenants pay your debt and expenses, and the property appreciates. What a great wealth builder! But this strategy also requires working with tenants and becoming a property manager. If you can hang in there over time, you'll realize a profit and eventually build the wealth you want.

However, be sure to consider the reward-to-work ratio. Going for greater profits can require a lot more work. That's why I have another rule of business: The more people involved, the more complicated everything is. That means the more tenants you have, the more work you'll have. You see, the actual house or duplex never calls to ask me for anything; it's the people living in the house or duplex who call and demand a lot of my time. The same is true for you and your time.

Don't confuse property ownership with property management. Property ownership is what you're going for; property management is what drives most people crazy. Similarly, although rehabbing properties can turn into a profitable business, it's managing the contractors that drives most investors crazy. Make sure that you have good systems in place to manage your people and processes.

High Return on Investment

With three wealth engines running, your possible return on investment is high, or, as I like to say, infinite. These are your engines: You own properties that appreciate, you'll realize tax advantages, and you'll use other people's money to make it all happen. All this leads to endless ROI possibilities.

Ways to Make Money in Real Estate

The following sections give you expanded ideas for making money in a variety of ways.

Buying, Renting, and/or Rehabbing Properties

You can build your real estate investing business by buying rental property and doing rehabs. I highly recommend hiring a manager, however, so that you're not involved in the day-to-day details. Instead, you manage the manager.

Wholesaling

To wholesale property, you find a good deal, put it under contract, advertise it for more money than you are paying, then close on it with the buyer at the same time that you close on it with the original seller. Wholesaling has distinct advantages: no buying, no borrowing money, and no dealing with tenants or contractors.

Lease Optioning

This involves leasing a property with the option to buy it at a fixed price, below market value. Lease optioning has become more and more popular. Twenty years ago, few cars were being leased; today about half of the cars on the road are leased. Lease optioning can answer many problems. For example, self-employed people who can't qualify for a mortgage can rent-to-own their home and new residents can rent-to-own while they take time to get settled in a new area.

Money Brokering

As a broker, you become the go-between for people who *have* money and people who *need* money, and you charge a fee to put them together, as most banks do. See the similarity? Banks take money from people who open savings and checking accounts, pay them a low interest rate for the use of their money, then turn around and lend that same money out at a much higher interest rate.

As a hard moneylender, you take on the role of the bank. You lend money on property, secured by real estate, and get paid for putting deals together. After about 10 years in business, many successful real estate investors become hard moneylenders.

Consulting

Once you've been in business for a few years, people ask you for advice. As a consultant, you can charge an hourly rate or a percentage of the profits if you help with a deal.

Property Management

Once you learn to manage rental property, you can do it for other people. Property managers charge from 5 percent to 10 percent of the gross rent, plus various fees.

Real Estate Agent

Real estate agents earn commissions from helping people buy and sell real estate, although it's not the same as being a real estate investor. There are advantages to being an agent (earning commissions, access to a real estate office and listing services, and ability to run comparable sales analyses), but I decided they were greatly outweighed by these disadvantages: licensing requirements, fees, long contracts, and lots of regulation. In addition, agents can't pay finder's fees to people who are not real estate agents, while investors can.

Mortgage Brokering

You can start your own brokerage business, or you can affiliate with brokers and receive a referral fee for every deal you send their way.

Establishing Affiliations

You can make connections with construction companies or affiliate with contractors, title companies, and closing agencies to get a referral fee for every job you send their way. Or you can start your own company to provide these services. For all affiliations, be sure to check on the legalities in your area, and disclose your affiliations in writing to everyone involved in what you are doing.

Developing Land

Buy land, add zoning and sewers, perhaps even homes, and then sell everything for much more than you paid for it. Two of the most lucrative businesses in the world are buying whiskey by the bottle and selling it by the shot, and buying land by the acre and selling it by the lot. Real estate developers make a lot of money because instead of doing one deal at a time, they deal with multiples.

Presenting Seminars and Writing Books

When you've gone to a seminar given by an expert, have you ever wondered, "If this person is making so much money in real estate, why is he selling books and courses and doing seminars?" I can only speak for myself, but the main reason I write books and lead seminars is that I like doing them. I suggest that you never do anything you don't like to do.

Although I do make some money from my books and seminars, I made more money from one real estate deal last year than I did from all my books and course sales in the last five years. And I've got three best-selling real estate books. Besides, I take almost all the proceeds from my books and courses, and donate them directly to charity. That's why I'm so motivated—because I like to help people in as many ways as I can. Again, it is easier to make more money from a $200,000 home than from a $20 book.

Buying Properties Preconstruction

When you buy preconstructed properties, you put down a deposit before anything gets built. Suppose you have contracted to buy a preconstructed house and the developer raises the prices within a year. You can sell your contract for more than you secured it for. In this area of investing, especially beware of supply and demand. Also recognize you have capital tied up in your deposit. Most important of all, to minimize your risk, make sure you feel comfortable dealing with the builder/developer over time.

What Kind of Properties?

Should you invest in single-family homes, duplexes, apartment buildings, condominiums, shopping centers, office buildings, land, or trailers? This 40-Day Plan has worked in nearly every community with every type of property. Keep your investor's eyes open. Remember, someone's going to buy that property you're considering; someone's going to sell it; someone's going to move into it.

Staying narrow, deep, and focused brings success in any business. It's competitive out there. Most investors select one or two types of property and one geographic area to specialize in. I began specializing in single-family homes and duplexes in a certain area of Nashville, Tennessee, and it's worked well for me. I have a friend who specializes in small apartment buildings; another who just does preconstruction on condos; another who just does new construction in Las Vegas; another who just does small commercial properties in his area. I highly recommend that you stay narrow, deep, and focused to keep your possibilities limitless.

This Is Your 40-Day Plan

Remember, the plan you're about to follow is based on a 5-hour to 10-hour work week (that is, if you're working 5 days a week, 2 hours a day at real estate, that's 10 hours a week). The question is this: Do you have 10 hours a week to devote to building a new business? Almost everybody does. If your life is already full with a family and job, you might have to take it a bit slower and devote just five hours a week. Achieving success will take you a bit longer, but you can still succeed in real estate using this approach.

Maybe you're already involved in real estate investing. Great! If you're working at it full-time, you can follow this success plan quite fast—perhaps going through it in 20 days instead of 40. If you feel stuck, use this plan to refocus and get back on track. This action plan will ensure that you focus on activities that will bring you success and financial rewards.

The first step is to commit to the 40-Day Plan by signing below:

I, _____ (your name) _____ , commit to

following these action plans for ___ days. Starting Date _____

Author's Note

This book is filled with ideas that have worked for others and can work for you, too. Please only use the ideas that you feel absolutely comfortable with. All business, including real estate, should consist of win/win transactions. Help others and you shall win, too.

For those readers who think some of the material in this book in simple or basic, my question to you is this: Are you practicing these methods? It's usually the simple procedures that bring you the most success!

Happy Investing.

Goal Setting, Part 1

Before we delve into the "how" of real estate investing, think about the "why." Where do you want to be three years from now? Five years from now? Ten years from now?

What Motivates You?

The number one determinant of your success in real estate investing is your desire: your motivation as reflected in your goals and your plan. Many people think success in real estate investing hinges on your understanding of contracts, laws, and financial concepts. I don't believe that. The most successful people I've met have a lot of desire. Nothing stopped them.

As a matter of fact, many of the supersuccessful investors actually don't know everything about real estate investing. Many aren't familiar with a lot of the concepts you'll get to know in this book, such as wholesaling, lease optioning, limited liability companies, advanced analysis, or different types of contracts. They simply have a lot of desire; they go out and make things happen; they don't worry about it—they just keep working their Action Plan. When I started in real estate investing, I didn't know these things either. But I did enough activities to experience enough successes.

The most important part of your real estate investing career is desire and motivation—whether you've been in real estate for 10 years, or you're just starting out, or you've spent the last 10 years just thinking about getting started.

Where Do You Get Your Advice?

As you get started actually doing the activities of real estate and applying this 40-Day Plan, I suggest you share your desires and motivations with people. Be prepared for all kinds of responses, because you will get them. Probably, you have people in your life who support what you do, and others who ridicule you no matter what; some have a sense of humor and will make fun of your ambitions while still others will ignore them, thinking they're just more of your dreams.

For fun, take the most skeptical person's comment, write it down, and then, six months to a year from now, when you've closed on your first deal and are making money, give them some of your money. Just give them a $500 check, saying, "You laughed at me when I said I was getting into real estate. Well, I just did a deal and made $7,000." Then, see what they say. They'll be shocked. Suddenly, they'll become interested in real estate investing.

Most people get advice from *three groups* of people. It's important that you know this as you seek help building your business.

Group One includes people who have absolutely no clue what they're talking about, but love to give advice. Unfortunately, these are the people (often family members) from whom we get most of our advice. They love to say things like, "That doesn't work. You're crazy. That's another scam." They have a lot of negative things to say, but they haven't done any real estate investing themselves. So when you hear their advice, mentally put them in Group One, and don't pay any attention to what they're saying.

Group Two is made up of people who've tried something, failed miserably, and love to tell you about it. They might say, "I bought a real estate course from a TV show. I tried real estate, and it doesn't work, so don't you do it!" That's when you ask them, "How long did you stick with it?" You'll probably find out they never even read the course. These people remind me of a friend who's been divorced four times and still loves to give relationship advice. So notice when your advice is coming from someone in Group Two, and don't pay much attention.

Group Three, the last group we get our advice from (and the smallest group), is made up of experts. Those are people who've been doing something successfully for over five years. I hope that's why you bought this book—because you want advice from an expert. I've been investing in real estate for over 12 years, and people consider me an expert.

Whatever you do, make sure you're paying attention only to advice from Group Three—the experts.

Do What Works

As you launch your real estate investing career, notice what is working for you. I challenge you: If one thing works, do more of it. I go around the county, and I meet people who don't follow this seemingly commonsense philosophy. For example, one guy said, "I called my real estate agent, and he found a deal. I made $80,000!"

"Did you call him again?"

"No."

"Do you talk to him anymore?"

"No."

"Have you got any other agents working for you?"

"No."

It's human nature. All of us do something that works really well, and then we quit. For example, have you ever been in a relationship, ended it, gotten involved with someone else, and realized how good the first one was?

I quit doing something that worked in my fifth year in real estate. I had been wholesaling properties at a rate of about one a week. I made a lot of money. It was unbelievable. I wasn't fighting with contractors; I didn't have to deal with tenants. My workload went down. I had free time. Then, the next year, I got into property management. I had 18 employees and was busy all the time. It was stressful. My company was very good, but we made no money. Still, I did that for two years. And I wholesaled only a handful of properties during those years, because I was so busy doing something that didn't really work well. So, if you're doing something that works, do more of it.

> **Warning: People love to complicate things. They want advanced techniques and fancy maneuvers. I could give you 300 pages of advanced information. But it's doing the basics that makes money. The problem is that most people are unwilling to do the basics. Stay with the simple. Do the simple things, and you'll be successful.**

Mark a Spot

I encourage you to do the following exercise to demonstrate how your mind works and how you can put it to work for you in setting your goals.

Relax. Stare at the wall. Without moving your shoulders or straining your neck, look as far to the left as you can. Mentally mark the spot on the wall. Look forward. Then again, without moving your shoulders or straining your neck, look to the right as far as you can. Mentally mark the spot on the wall. Remember those spots. Turn forward again.

Do the same thing again, but this time you can move your body. Turn all the way to the left, moving your shoulders, turning as far as you can, and mentally mark the spot you can see on the wall. Look forward once more. This time, look left again, keeping your shoulders still, as you did the first time. Notice the spot you're looking at. Is it farther away than the first spot?

What's the difference between the two? You set a higher goal. Your subconscious mind realized that you could see farther than you did the first time. That's the only difference. Your subconscious makes a record of everything you say, do, and take in.

Use this mind-stretching activity in your goal setting. Set your goal today, then after doing real estate for one to three months, come back, review your goal, and notice how much farther you see.

Included in these 40-Days to Success is the opportunity to meet a lot of other successful real estate investors. You'll be getting to know people just like you, who had no experience in real estate; they were just beginners at one point, and now they're creating a lot of wealth. Their insights will help you realize your potential.

The Secret System

I'm sharing with you a secret system for becoming a successful real estate investor. It took me seven years to discover it. Most people do real estate backwards. They try to figure out what they're going to do with the property before they even have a property. But the secret is this: First, find a motivated seller. It doesn't matter what you're going to do with the property (wholesale, fix and sell, lease option, rent). In every case, you have to find a good deal. Making money in real estate hinges on that. Second, analyze the deal. Third, once it's a deal, immediately control it by putting it under contract. Then, you have time to figure out how you'll use your deal to make money.

That's the three-part system. Most people worry about the end before they do the beginning. They analyze themselves out of everything.

Right Attitude—No Emotions

Real estate investing is a business, but it doesn't have to be an emotional one. Try to remove all of your emotions from your activities. It's just real estate; no one will die if you mess up (unlike performing open-heart surgery). I know it's human nature to worry. But realize that the most successful business people remove their emotions when doing transactions. I suggest you not become attached to the property. Don't get attached to the neighborhood. Real estate is just numbers and contracts and systems. If you keep working the system, you'll eventually purchase some property. If you don't believe me, you can keep yourself busy with worry and analysis. Be assured of one thing: Worry will paralyze you.

> The Small Business Administration did a study of all the reasons people succeed in business. It considered education, background, experience, family, where they lived, and what type of business they started. The study concluded that the number one determinant of success was desire. Desire, motivation, and goals are all different sides of the same thing.

All success takes is the right mental attitude—realizing that real estate is just a business, and you're just conducting business transactions. Don't allow yourself to get emotionally attached to the properties or the deals. And remember, you don't have to know everything to get started.

DAY 1   Action Plan

It's Up to You to Make It Happen!

Write down what motivates you. Remember, there are no wrong answers. Whatever you desire is correct.

✔ Why are you interested in real estate? What motivated you to purchase this book and learn more about real estate?

_____

_____

_____

_____

Here are some common answers to these questions: make more money, be my own boss, become financially independent, be able to take more vacations, get rid of my boss, tell my boss I'm leaving and feel good about it, create wealth for future generations of my family, build retirement savings, take control, make up for losses in the stock market.

✔ Whatever your answer is, write it down on a card and look at it every day.

✔ In the exercise above, you might have written down, "I want to make more money." That's an excellent goal; there's nothing wrong with making more money. The question is this: What are you going to do with the money? So if you wrote down, "I want to make more money," be more specific and write down exactly what you're going to do with it. For example, are you going to pay off some debt, take a trip, buy a toy? Whatever it is, write it down.

_____

_____

✔ Now it's time to get specific about how much money you want to make. Be realistic. If you're just getting started, maybe you want to make an extra $10,000 to $20,000 to $150,000 this year. Or an extra $2,000 a month.

Go back to the particulars. What will you do with that money, if you could work part-time and make an extra few thousand dollars a month? What would you do with your extra cash? How would it change your lifestyle? Write down what difference that would make for you and your family.

_____

_____

_____

_____

_____

✔ Next, find a specific example of a motivating factor—what your success would look like exactly. For example, if your goal is to take a vacation with your family, then find a picture of the island location, and post it in your kitchen or bathroom. If you're motivated to make more money, write down the amount, and describe what the money is for. Look at your written statement often. Perhaps you want to buy a new car. Locate a picture of your dream car, put that picture on your desk, and look at it every day.

Determining that motivation will remind you of why you're getting into real estate.

Remember, your number one determinant of success is your desire, your motivation. This visual reminder will encourage you weeks down the road. If you're having a bad moment, don't get frustrated. Just reread that card with your goal written on it, and look at the picture of what you want. You'll be motivated again to keep on going. It will reignite you.

Goal Setting, Part 2

You've written down your main desire, what motivates you. The next step is to address a common problem. Many successful real estate investors never reward themselves. They keep making money, but they never really enjoy it. So today, you'll explore your perfect day of play. After that, you'll envision your perfect day of work.

Your Perfect Day of Play

You might be saying to yourself that this book is supposed to be about real estate investing. Why are we doing all this touchy-feely stuff? Because you have to know when you've reached success. If you skipped over Day 1 exercises, go back and do them. They are extremely important.

Your ideas may start to flow if you read how a few other people have described their days. Felicia's perfect day starts with reading the Bible, exercising, and eating a breakfast of fresh fruits. Then, she gets a spa treatment from the Mandarin Oriental in Miami, Florida. After a one-hour nap, she gets another spa treatment. Then, she eats a special lunch of fresh fish and steamed vegetables, prepared in front of her by a private chef. Lunch is followed by a foot massage. She walks on the beach during the afternoon. Any kinks from her walk are worked out by another full-body spa treatment. She follows that by a period of meditation. One last spa treatment ends the day.

What would this cost? To fly to the spa, $300. A night in a nice hotel, $200. A good massage, $150. So with the multiple spa treatments and private chef, Felicia can have her perfect day for about $2,000.

To start to make this dream a reality, Felicia has to write this down. Then, she needs to keep what she wrote in sight for motivation. The final step comes after her first real estate deal. She must pay herself first. If she makes $8,000, she'll take $2,000 to enjoy her perfect day of play. When she does, guess what she'll want to do? She'll do more real estate deals and come up with another perfect day of play.

The biggest problem with real estate investors who make a lot of money is that they're so busy working at their business that they never take any time off to enjoy the fruits of their labors. You need a strong commitment to pay yourself first and play; we tend to pay everybody else first. Of course, you need to make sure your bills are paid. But be sure to reward yourself.

You're making a big commitment of yourself and your time to get into real estate investing. You can make it happen, but remember why you're getting into real estate in the first place. I hope it's to have fun and make money.

Once you get rolling, take a day of play every time you finalize two to five deals. Make it part of your success plan. I promise you that these days will help you relax and clear your mind. As a result, you'll be able to do even more deals when you return.

Your Perfect Day of Work

Most people just jump into real estate without spending time exploring their goals. I travel around the country and ask thousands of real estate investors, "What's your plan? What are your goals?" Most of them say, "I'm just going to get into real estate, and something good is going to happen."

Well, that's not a bad plan. It's better than most people's plans, which are no plans at all. They just go to work, watch TV, and go to sleep. They're not willing to do something different. They won't pick up a book, go to a seminar, or take a risk. That's why I commend anyone who says, "My plan is to get into real estate, and something good will happen."

You are different. You've picked up this book and are willing to try something. You're in the top 3 percent of the population. Most people go through life doing the same thing over and over again without goals or plans. They're negative; they doubt everything. But you're making the effort to learn something new. You're following a success plan. Congratulations!

But let's make an even better plan.

Everything in your life results from thought. Everything in your life is an idea. The house you live in resulted from someone's thought. The car you drive started as an idea. Someone thought about a car, drew it, built it, and made it a reality. Your real estate business is something you're thinking about; you're wise to be thinking about your success in it.

Maybe you haven't thought this through entirely for yourself. Take a few minutes to picture in your mind what you'd like to accomplish. That's what you'll spend Day 2 doing.

Review, Reenvision, Rewrite

After you learn the entire 40-Day Plan for Success in Real Estate Investing, it's important to go back and review. Be sure to revisit your goals and perfect days of work and play, because you could realize that you have much more opportunity than you'd first imagined. With any and all limits lifted, you can set your sights even higher.

Make reviewing your goals a regular part of your work routine. Review your plans every few months, updating them as necessary. You will start achieving success, and your objectives will grow more exciting and fun. If you're making $2,000 to $8,000 a month today and you start making $20,000 a month through success in real estate investing, your lifestyle and goals will likely change.

For the first five years I was in real estate, I never thought about any of this goal setting or forward thinking. My business was operating very well in Nashville, Tennessee. I was working between 50 and 75 hours a week and feeling stressed out. One day, I decided to stop all my activities and analyze my business. I read several books and came across this idea about creating a perfect day of play and work. So one day, I went out on a limb, and decided to work seven hours instead of ten. You see, I had limited my imagination.

Then, I read a few more books and reenvisioned my perfect days of work and play. I discovered that my perfect day of work expanded to doing my business from anywhere, being able to travel constantly, living by the beach, and having assistants handle details of the business that I don't enjoy, such as accounting and bookkeeping. I would do deals all over the United States and in some foreign countries. My income would double, enabling me to donate to charities and help people.

When I wrote down everything I wanted, it all seemed unrealistic. Then two years later, I moved to South Beach, Florida, and today I am making my vision a reality. I live by the beach with a view of the ocean. I have assistants who handle the details I'm not good at. I'm doing real estate deals all over the United States. My income has more than doubled. And even though I work hard some weeks, I'm traveling constantly and taking a lot of time off—usually two months a year.

A few years ago, I would have thought having all of this impossible. But I believe if you write down your dreams and think about what you really want to happen, even if you don't expect your dreams to come true, they will. Revisit your goals and look at them often.

Many of my students make more than $25,000 a month. I can assure you that their goals and perfect days of work and play have changed a lot over time. You could make enough money to hire someone to worry. Some people like to worry. Why not pay them to do it for you? Certainly, make it a goal to have enough money that you can hire someone to tell you how to have more fun!

The Mind Is a Powerful Tool

While setting your goals, don't forget to put your mind to work. Here are two examples of people who did.

In my three-day boot camp trainings, students have a lot of time to do intensive goal setting. Most participants state a realistic goal of making an extra $3,000 to $5,000 a month doing real estate. This would net them more income in a year than the average family of four makes annually. Not bad for a part-time job!

At one of my boot camps last summer, Brad boldly set his monthly goal at $30,000 a month. He had no experience in real estate. But after learning about wholesaling and lease optioning, he was confident he could make that much from the beginning by doing real estate deals full-time.

The other participants laughed. They'd all spent three days learning about real estate investing, hearing about successes—and they still thought it was impossible to make that much a month from the get-go. I cautioned him, too, suggesting he might want to be more conservative and allow more time to get there.

Brad emphatically held to his goal, declaring that, after allowing himself three months to get things going, he planned to make $30,000 a month. "Why not?" he challenged. After three months in investing, Brad called me. Instead of making $30,000 that month, he had made $42,000 from wholesaling one property. Eight months later, Brad has consistently been making between $30,000 and $50,000 a month. Since he started, there's not been one month he's made less than $30,000. Today, his average is creeping even higher. He's wholesaling high-end properties and doing high-end lease options. It's fascinating to watch people set goals and meet them.

Another example is a woman who came to one of my seminars and said her only goal was to make $5,000 in real estate. That's it. Is that a bad goal? No! Whatever your goals are, they're right for you. I asked her why she wanted to make $5,000. She replied, "Well, I really don't need to make that much. If I made $3,000, I'd be happy." So she set her goal even higher than what she wanted.

She'd just become divorced and was a single mom. She said her ex-husband never took them on vacation so her goal was to take her 10-year-old son on a vacation to the Grand Canyon. Eight weeks after the seminar, she found a little house in Tennessee, wholesaled it, and made $5,800 in profit.

Two weeks later, she and her son flew out to the Grand Canyon. She called me from the rim of the canyon, crying with joy, telling me she'd met her goal. They spent a full week there taking helicopter rides, going up and down the canyon on mules, and having a good time. Her son had never been on a vacation in his life.

They came home, and she never did another real estate deal. She's a teacher and didn't have that much interest in real estate. That trip was her goal. And she proudly met it.

Setting Step-by-Step Goals

I'm a big believer in motivation and goal setting, both short-term and long-term. But none of that will help you unless you do something to make it happen. These 40 Days to Success will be pivotal in realizing your goals. It tells you what to do *today*. That's your most important question: What are you going to do today? What are you going to do tomorrow? What are you going to do next week?

Your goals need to extend beyond how much money you're going to make to include the activities that will help you make your end-goal. This book will walk you through the how of real estate investing, step by step.

DAY 2   Action Plan

It's Up to You to Make It Happen!

✔ Take three minutes to write down what your perfect day of play would be. If you had two days and an extra $2,000 to just blow and have fun, what would you do? The more detail you write down, the better.

Where would you go?

_____

_____

What would you do?

_____

_____

_____

_____

Who would go with you?

_____

_____

What would you eat?

_____

_____

✔ Write down what your perfect day of work would be. Imagine you've been in real estate for a few years. It's very important to take a few minutes *right now* to create this picture.

Think in limitless possibilities. You might think you can live and work in only one place, or do only a certain type of real estate, or make only a certain amount of money. Ask yourself, "Why?" I'm not asking you to be unrealistic or be a crazy dreamer, although there's nothing wrong with that either! Let yourself dream.

What does your day look like?

_____

_____

_____

Where are you?

_____

_____

With whom are you working?

_____

_____

How much money do you make?

_____

What kind of real estate do you own?

_____

_____

What kind of deals are you working on?

_____

_____

_____

Building Your Team

Start thinking about your business team. Unfortunately, most real estate investors are a team of one. They're entrepreneurial, like Rambo standing in the field with a machine gun in his hand and the entire Russian army coming at him with tanks and airplanes. He's by himself, and you think you're by yourself. You're not! That's why you want to build your team.

Team Members Who Share Your Belief

Be sure the people you choose have experience in the type of deals you want to do—people who've worked with investors. For example, some real estate agents will tell you that it's illegal to wholesale property (it's not). I've already covered the types of people we get advice from. You're looking for people from Group Three, the experts who've really done what you're talking about.

Build your team through good references. Ask successful real estate investors in your area for referrals. Go to www.sheminrealestate.com, for a list of real estate associations all around the country, to find other investors. Choose people who are pros or people new to the business who are hungry and willing to grow and work with you.

Present Your Business

Before making calls, have your plan ready so that you can clearly communicate how serious you are about building your business. Posture your business in a strong, positive way.

Most investors plead. They call up a potential team member and say, "Golly, gee, I'm thinking about doing some real estate investing, and I don't know what I'm doing. But would you please work with me? Help!" That doesn't sound impressive. Who wants to go into business with a pleader?

Use your goal setting, and plan what kind of business you envision. So if you're starting out and want to do 10 deals a year, tell that contact person, "I'm a new real estate investor, but I have a plan, and I'm going to do 10 deals this year. I'd love to work with you. Maybe you can help me buy or sell properties.

"Would you be interested in building a long-term business? I'm committed to doing this for 5 to 10 years. That's a lot of houses. I'm building a big business, and I'm looking for a few good people to work with. Are you interested?" Most people will respond positively to that.

Build a Business through Referrals

My business approach is that I help people. If other people have a problem, you can help them. If they don't have a problem, you can't help them. If you find people who want to sell their houses, but they're not motivated enough to build in a profit for you, refer them to a real estate agent you've partnered with.

Your real estate agent can help you help people. Obviously, the more you help them, the more they help you. They'll think of you when they come across a motivated seller. If you treat people well, they will start calling you with deals. This is how I find almost all my deals now.

It takes about three to five years to get to this point; that's why I recommend you commit to doing this for at least five years before you decide whether it's working for you. In any business, 60 percent to 80 percent of the business comes from referrals. Think about that when you're calling people and working with them. Take care of them, and they'll take care of you.

Who Should Be on Your Team?

Now that you're starting a real estate investing business, you are always looking for three things: motivated sellers, buyers, and sources of money. Each team member does more than one thing for you. In addition to their specialties, they can be sources of these three things you're always looking for. You're helping them build their businesses, and they're helping you build your business.

Real Estate Agent

Real estate agents can scour the MLS for deals and run comparable sales analyses. They are a source of buyers, motivated sellers, and people with money: the three lists that you'll want to build to grow your business.

To find agents to partner with, ask a few people at your real estate association, look through the newspaper, and call two to five real estate agents who seem to be active. Ask them, "Do you work with investors?" Once you find one agent who does, then you'll find the rest of your team.

Mortgage Broker

Investor loans are more difficult than conventional loans. Having a mortgage broker on your team can be a big advantage.

People with Money

Find people who have easily verifiable income (W-2 rather than self-employed) and borrow funds from them or use their credit. Whatever you don't have, find someone who has it.

Don't Worry, Be Happy

I'm a worrier. Are you? After going to law school, I went from being a normal worrier to being paranoid! Then, I learned there is another way to look at things.

A few years ago, I noticed a young-looking man at the gym I went to in Nashville. He seemed really happy and was always smiling. I, on the other hand, was always worried about my real estate business—what might happen, what might not—and I couldn't concentrate.

Finally, I went up to this guy and said, "I've noticed you seem so happy all the time. What's your secret?" He said, "How old do you think I am?" I said, "About 28, you can't be a day over 30. In fact, you look to be about 25."

He said, "I'm 54." I made him pull out his driver's license to prove it; it seemed impossible.

He said, "I'll tell you my secret: I don't worry."

"How could that be?" I argued. "There's always something to worry about!"

He explained, "Many years ago, I figured something out. Anything I was going to worry about, if I could do something about it, I'd do it and then not worry. If there was nothing I could do about it, worry didn't help. Therefore, I never worry." And he was a security guard at a bank. He didn't have a great job, nor did he make a ton of money.

What do most people do? Fret and worry. You surmise that if you can't do anything about it, the least you can do is worry. Or perhaps you could do something about it, like pick up the phone and call an expert to ask a question. But instead of doing that, you'll spend a week worrying. Or better yet, you'll ask people who have no clue of what they're talking about (Group One) for their advice, so they can help you worry.

From now on, will you stop worrying about anything? At least try to do less worrying.

Title Agent/Escrow Agent/Closing Agent

Having a title agent familiar with you and your business can be helpful at closing, especially when you do wholesaling.

Real Estate Lawyer

A real estate lawyer will help you keep what you earn, protecting you from potential lawsuits. Your lawyer will set up your corporations and look over your contracts, partner agreements, and other documents before you sign them.

Accountant

One of the biggest surprises for me in real estate is the amount of work required to keep up with the money flowing in and out—where it's coming from and where it's going. Like most investors starting out, I tried to do it on my own. It was a small disaster.

I recommend putting a system in place. Open a separate bank account to keep your business transactions apart from personal funds. Have a separate folder for every property. Quickbooks can perform well for budgets, or hire a professional bookkeeping service. Give them your receipts throughout the year; then at tax time, your return will be ready. Make sure your accountants own real estate, too, and understand what you're doing. They'll keep up with the laws better. Choose a good one through a referral source you trust.

Almost everyone I know who has been successful in real estate investing for over seven years has been through a full IRS audit. You'd better have good records and be ready.

You might think hiring a professional to handle your bookkeeping, accounting, and taxes will cost you money, but it will actually save you money. Remember, if all you did was find one more deal with that extra time, the service was worth it. The cost of paying the person is not important; look at the cost of *not* having the right professional help: stress, aggravation, not having good records, and lost time to find deals.

Appraiser

At times, you'll want to hire an appraiser to handle your transactions smoothly.

Contractor

When you're analyzing deals, you'll need a contractor to assign a cost to any repairs needed. Use a contractor rather than a home inspector. Although home inspectors provide an important service when you're buying your own home, they aren't effective for your purposes in real estate investing. If you hire a home inspector for $300 to $500, all you get is a report that says what the problems are. That's good information, but you need a number. You need to know how much it will cost to fix the problems. So when you buy property for your business, hire a contractor who can not only find the problems, but can also give you a receipt detailing the costs to repair them.

Business People

Choose sharp people to participate on your board of directors or to consult with you. Take them out to lunch once a month. Tell them you're starting a business and would like their valuable input. People love to help other people. Ask them, "Could I run a few ideas by you? I'd be very appreciative of your time. Maybe down the road I'll be able to pay you when my business grows. I really respect you. Would you help me?"

Good business people will be able to look at what you're doing, and in 30 minutes or over dinner, they'll be able to give you a few ideas that literally could change your whole business. It'll probably be some of the best consulting you'll ever get. And you're actually doing them a favor, by giving them the opportunity to help someone.

I went to the president of the biggest bank in my town, someone I didn't really know, and asked him to help me with my business. He would sit down with me every so often for 30 minutes and ask, "What are you doing? Why don't you do this? Go meet these people. Go over here—he's buying property; she's selling property." He really helped my business.

Insurance Broker

You'll need to carry proper insurance on your properties and your business.

Other Real Estate Investors

Find the three most active investors in your town and take them to lunch. In fact, that's your Action Plan for Day 3. They are big buyers; they'll buy anything you can find. Because they're out looking for deals, they'll find deals they don't want—they can give them to you. Third, they have money. They might finance deals for you.

People always ask me how I got into real estate. It was completely by accident. I had no desire or interest to be in real estate. That is, until I met a gentleman in Nashville, Tennessee, who had a lot of rental properties. He had no formal education or background in real estate. I met him in his dumpy office. He didn't have a computer. He still doesn't. But he had over 100 houses in Nashville, paid for, and his net worth was in the multimillions. He was making between $500,000 and $1 million a year off his rental properties.

When I met him, he opened up his frayed ledger and showed me all the properties he'd accumulated over the previous 20 years. He didn't start in real estate until his mid-fifties, so you beginners still have time. In the beginning, he worked really hard, but for the last seven years, he had been taking seven months vacation each year.

That's when he turned to me and asked, "Robert, how's your job?"

I said, "Not as good as yours!" I recognized this golden opportunity. So I asked if I could talk with him more about real estate investing. I took him to lunch. He spent two hours with me, telling me what he did. Then I met other investors, took them to lunch, and learned what they did. That's how I got started.

You're starting your business; you need to ask people for help. Tell them you're building your business and are looking for deals. If you ask enough people, you'll find them. Even go to the busiest investors in your town, people who are doing 200 deals a year, and say, "I'm just starting out and would like to get some deals." You might be surprised; they just might pass along some deals to you.

Not long ago, I lease optioned five properties to David in Nashville. Now, I knew exactly what those properties were worth, but I let him lease option them from me for almost no money down at 78 cents on the dollar. So, for example, one of the duplexes was worth $100,000, and I let him have it for $78,000. I gave him terms. Now he manages them, rents them, and makes money.

Why did I, a hard-core, seasoned investor, lease option them with such generous terms? There's only one reason I did it for David and didn't for anyone else. He asked. He said, "Hey Robert, I'm starting in real estate; you've got a bunch of property. Do you have any you want to peel off?"

I was willing to work with David because I wasn't interested in the five properties anymore. I'd bought them way below market five years earlier, I'd rented them and was willing to sell them below market to avoid listing them, paying commissions, and scaring my tenants away. And I made money.

So ask people. Tell them you're looking for deals.

In school, if you ask a lot of questions, people think you're dumb. Now that you're an adult, asking for help is a sign of strength. Most people want to help. You just have to ask.

Do you need money? Ask people if they'll help you finance a deal. Do you need good credit? Ask people who already have it, if you can use their credit and split the deal. If you're looking for real estate deals, call other investors and ask them. Call business people to ask for advice in starting your business.

What do you want? Ask for it! That's your homework.

Is Money the Root of All Evil?

Here is one of the most misquoted statements from the Bible: "Money is the root of all evil." That is not the exact quote. It's actually "the love of money is the root of all evil." It means loving money for the sake of money. You've got to prepare yourself mentally if you're going to make a lot of money. You might change. People around you might change in their attitude toward you. Are you prepared for this? A lot of people aren't.

Take a few minutes to examine your ideas about money and wealth. Where do they come from? Consider the word "money"; what comes to mind? Consider the word "wealth"; what comes to mind? Consider the word "rich"; what comes to mind? Consider the word "landlord"; what comes to mind? Write your ideas down.

Others' responses to these words include: doing what you want and when you want; easy living; the way it's supposed to be; abundance; inner and outer wealth. On the negative side, people think having wealth means having "friends" appear out of the woodwork to borrow money; the responsibility of money; greed; money running through your fingers like water; losing what you have; getting it the easy way; slumlord; squeezing the last dollar out of every rental property; just plain dumb luck.

I promise you this. Once you start making money in real estate, people will say you're just lucky. They don't realize the time you spent learning and doing—looking at deals for 80 hours before you found that lucky deal.

Examining your ideas about money and wealth is important because after you get into real estate, you'll start making money and could even become very wealthy.

What Is Your Hour Worth?

How much do you think your hour is worth? Most people are brought up thinking their time is worth $7 to $14 an hour. Many people whose parents worked in a management job making $40,000 to $60,000 a year think that's what their year is worth. You only have one asset in your life—time. How are you going to spend it? And what are you expecting to get for it?

As you start your own business, determine what your hour is worth. If you think it's worth $10 an hour, that's what you'll make. You'll do activities in your real estate business that support that rate, like painting, drywalling, and cleaning. There's nothing wrong with this if you have to do it in the beginning of your business, but keep in mind what your hour is worth.

If you determine that your hour is worth $200, you won't spend time on activities that won't support that rate. Instead of painting and cleaning carpets, you'll be out finding deals. That's where the real money is.

Constantly remind yourself what your hour is worth. Check your activity, and ask yourself what it would cost to hire someone else to do it. For instance, if you're doing the painting yourself, find out how much you can hire a painter for. Say it's $10 an hour—then why are you doing the painting? Maybe you don't like bookkeeping. What can you hire a good bookkeeper for? Look at what you're doing, what your hour is worth, and where you got your ideas of what your time is worth.

What Size— Small, Medium, or Large?

Do you want a small business, a medium business, or a big business? Keep in mind that little businesses make a little money, medium businesses make medium money, and big businesses make big money. Does that change your mind? So let me ask it a different way: Do you want to make big money?

For many years, I had one or two real estate agents looking for deals for me. Today, I have about 25 real estate agents looking for deals for me. I have eight mortgage people whom I do business with—they're out there looking for deals for me. It's the same with other people on my team.

Don't get overextended right out of the gate. You want to start out focused, narrow, and deep. But have an end goal. How many people do you want looking for deals for you? If one real estate agent is finding you one deal every six months, for example, then why not get six agents looking for deals for you?

DAY 3   Action Plan

It's Up to You to Make It Happen!

Begin thinking about who's going to be on your team and start finding them. Over the next 10 to 20 days, you'll be building your team as you're completing the other activities.

✔ Find other real estate investors. How? Go to your local real estate association. Look in the newspaper, in the section called Investment Properties. Find three to five investors who've been doing real estate for over five years.

✔ Invite them to lunch. Ask them a series of questions:

How did you get started?

_____

_____

What kind of real estate are you doing?

_____

_____

What would you do differently?

_____

_____

What would you recommend for someone like me who's just starting out, or doing it part-time (whichever your situation is)?

_____

_____

Ask for recommendations of attorneys, contractors, and so forth.

_____

_____

What contracts are you using? List them.

_____

_____

What's the hardest part of your business?

_____

_____

If they're having trouble finding deals, maybe you can help them find deals and wholesale to them.

Remember, you're always building your seller's list, buyer's list, and sources of money list. One of the biggest obstacles to success in real estate is money. Investors you meet might partner with you to buy properties.

✔ Meet and invite to lunch one investor every week.

_____

Foreclosures, Part 1

Congratulations on setting up a proper mind-set. You're starting to think about your team and meeting people. It's time to find a motivated seller. That's what it's all about!

As you start looking for deals, you'll first learn all the ways to find motivated sellers—that's how you find a deal—then you'll follow the daily activities so you don't have to think or worry about outcomes. Finally, you'll learn how to analyze the deals you've found and put them under contract.

What Makes a Seller Motivated?

The key to making money in real estate is buying property below market value. What motivates people to sell real estate for below market? I don't know, and it doesn't matter. Years ago, I gave up trying to figure out why people do things. People don't make sense.

How much time do you spend worrying and thinking about why people do things or don't? It's not a very good use of your time. Let's get something out of the way right now. People can be very strange. Why don't more people do real estate investing? I don't know. Why do people smoke cigarettes? I have no idea. Why do people not wear their seatbelts? Beats me. What people do and don't do doesn't make much sense, so don't spend your time trying to figure them out.

What motivates some people to sell their property for below market? Although it certainly doesn't make sense to do so, people do it. I've done it—selling five duplexes for 22 percent below market. I'm not that greedy. I'm happy to give someone else a good deal. I made money. I'm happy to get 78 percent. The point is, don't worry about it.

New real estate investors worry, saying, "The real estate market has gone up. It's doubled in some cities in the last five years. It's very expensive. The real estate bubble is going to burst. Are there really any deals left?" Yes, there are always deals to be found.

When will people stop having financial troubles? Never. When will people stop getting divorced? Never. When will people stop dying? When will people start managing their rental property perfectly? When will people stop being transferred out of state or having to move quickly? When will they stop having to pay off debts quickly, after getting in over their heads? Never, never, never. So when will there stop being deals in real estate? Never. All these problems may motivate people to sell their real estate below market value.

Foreclosure rates are at their highest levels ever. Those people will lose their houses if they don't sell before the lenders foreclose on them. Their credit will be wrecked. That's motivation.

For the first time in many years, some banks and mortgage companies are shorting their mortgages. That means they are letting the mortgages be paid off for less than what they lent. That hasn't been common since the Depression. Why are they doing that? Somebody did an analysis and discovered that discounting them made more sense than keeping them on their books. Does that make sense? I don't know. But that's what banks want to do.

There will always be motivated sellers because of death, divorce, financial troubles, bad property management, property taxes, bad money management, the need to move quickly, and repairs that are needed (often not as costly as the current owner thinks). If you have a good contractor on your team, you can determine the extent of repairs needed. The house may look really bad, but will clean up well at a fraction of the expected cost.

Not too long ago, I was looking at a piece of real estate in Nashville. This particular property was a brand-new, beautiful, five-bedroom, three-bath executive home on five acres. It was easily worth $650,000. The newspaper ad said, "Must sell. Make offer." I asked what he'd like to get for it. He said, "I'd like $1." I laughed and said, "No, really, what do you want to sell your house for?"

Again, he said, "If you give me a contract for $1, I'll sign it."

"Why?"

"I'm getting divorced. I have to give my ex-wife half, and I can't wait to throw fifty cents at her."

So we wrote a contract for a dollar. The judge didn't accept it, but he did accept a contract for $340,000.

Why did the man want to sell his house for a dollar? Did it make sense? It did to him.

One time, someone practically gave me a house. He inherited it and didn't want it. He lived in New York and now owned a property in Tennessee, which he thought was a westward outpost. He asked me to please take the property—he couldn't understand how people lived south of Washington, D.C. He sold the property to me for 20 cents on the dollar, just because he didn't want it. It was a bother to him.

The first deal I did in South Beach, Florida, was with a gentleman who sold me a penthouse condominium at 30 percent below market. His only motivation was that he had too much money. He owned houses in Venice, New York, and California, and he got rid of this one like an old pair of shoes. He just didn't care. He even included the furniture, which was worth $150,000. He said, "Just take it; I don't need it."

Someone said I got lucky on that penthouse. I sure did—after looking at 50 of them. How many people are willing to call on 50 penthouses? How many people are willing to hear 49 "no's" and still make one more call? On the fiftieth, I got lucky. I promise you, if you stick with it and look for motivated sellers long enough, you'll get lucky too. You've just got to go out there and do the activity.

What Are Foreclosures?

One way to find motivated sellers is to delve into the foreclosure market. Foreclosures happen when people can't make the payments on a debt, and the lender tells them it is going to take the property to pay off the debt. These loans are secured by real estate. Foreclosures can also happen when people don't pay their bills and a creditor gets a lien or judgment against their real estate. These people are going to lose their property.

There are two ways to buy foreclosures: preforeclosures and tax sales.

Preforeclosures are deals from people who got a letter from the bank, saying the lender is about to foreclosure, unless they make the missing payments. That's one of the best foreclosure markets to work in because the owner still owns the house. Until the moment when the judge bangs her gavel finalizing the foreclosure, the people can still sell it. Of course, the debts have to be paid off—you can be the one to pay them.

Tax sales are from people who forgot to pay their taxes, such as property taxes. When buying property at tax sales, understand where the tax bill is in the order of debt on the property (see following subsection for explanation). In the order of debt, the government always gets paid first, to claim federal taxes, property taxes, and other federal liens from agencies such as the Drug Enforcement Administration (DEA), Justice Department and Bureau of Alcohol, Tobacco, and Firearms. Once one creditor forecloses, all debt below it gets wiped out. At the same time, any debt above it remains and must be paid.

Order of Debt

Be aware that there is an order of debt. Let's say you're going to buy a house for $500,000. You borrow $400,000. That's your first mortgage. The bankers tell you that you can get an equity line against your property and they lend you $50,000, so that you can go on vacation, make repairs, or go to school. That's your second mortgage. Next, let's say you paid a contractor to do some repairs on the house and then you got into a fight with him, so you didn't pay the bill. He can put a lien against your property, say $10,000, for the work he did. That debt becomes third in line. Then, you get in a car wreck, you hurt people, and you don't have enough insurance to pay the medical bills. The other people sue you, and their lawyer wins a judgment of $100,000 against you. You don't have the $100,000 in cash, so they put a lien against your property. This could go on and on and on. You could borrow more money from other people and stack up the debt on the house.

Who goes first in order of the liens? The government. The government will always be paid. So if you owe city or county or state taxes—they will go first above all the other debts. If you haven't paid your federal taxes, the IRS can place a lien against your house that trumps all others.

Let's say, for instance, you didn't pay your property taxes, and the city places a lien against your house—it's first in line. It's a governmental agency. If it forecloses on the house, then any further debt against the house gets wiped out.

If the property taxes were paid, but the bank with the $500,000 first mortgage forecloses because it wasn't paid, then all the liens below that will be wiped out.

Let's say everyone has been paid except for the $50,000 second mortgage. If the holder forecloses, every debt below that is wiped out, but the property still has a $400,000 mortgage and the $50,000 that's being foreclosed on.

I've worked on a house with seven mortgages. It was the third one that was being foreclosed on. You can buy whatever mortgage isn't being paid and then foreclose. Whenever you buy a mortgage, you step into the seller's shoes.

Governmental Agencies

There are other governmental agencies that may have an interest in people's property, such as the Drug Enforcement Administration going after drug dealers or the Justice Department going after white-collar crime, for example.

You can specialize in foreclosures in any one area. Remember, you're looking for motivated sellers. If the IRS has a lien against someone's house, that owner might be motivated to sell. If the DEA has put people in jail for dealing drugs and forces the owners to auction off their house, they may be motivated. You can start networking with the people in the governmental agencies and ask if they know of any real estate deals.

You might laugh this idea off, but consider what one deal is worth. If you find one house worth $100,000 for $60,000 and wholesale it for $80,000, then you'll make $20,000. Some people work all month or all year just to make $20,000.

I know a police officer who leads a SWAT team that busts crystal-meth labs. Members of his team deal with people who are making illegal drugs in their houses. Their biggest risk when they go in and arrest these people who make drugs, besides getting shot, is that the house could blow up because they're using highly volatile chemicals. They always have another team waiting outside in case the first team gets blown up. This officer and his team have busted more than 300 crystal-meth labs in this dangerous work.

In addition to being a police officer, my friend is a real estate investor on the side. He finds most of his deals through his day job. Of course, he discloses everything in writing, so that there's no conflict of interest. After a bust, he goes back to the people involved and makes an offer on the house that was once a meth lab. Then he wholesales it, making from $15,000 to $25,000 on every deal. He just retired from the police force at the age of 39 because he's made so much money from his real estate deals.

One of my best sources of deals has become police officers. Get to know them. If police officers or fire fighters refer business to you and you wholesale the house, pay them a generous finder's fee.

How to Find Foreclosures

- Partner with police officers or fire fighters to find deals.
- Get to know people at the tax office, foreclosure court, and other governmental agencies. When they find a deal, encourage them to call you.
- Look in the local and legal newspaper for foreclosures.

How to Work Foreclosures

Have you ever thought about going to a tax sale? Let me give you some hints. In every city, there are hundreds and sometimes thousands of people who don't pay their taxes. Then, the city auctions off their property. Sometimes, you get the property; sometimes you don't. But you get a lien against the property.

Here's how it works: If a house is worth $500,000, with a tax lien of $7,000 and you buy it at a tax sale, you can get the house for $7,000.

The laws in every city and state are different, so before you bid at a tax sale, find out exactly what you get. In some cities and states, if you pay the tax bill, you

Never buy or take an interest in a property without talking to a title insurance agent to make sure you can get clear title and title insurance.

Many people have bought properties at tax sales and learned afterwards that they can never get clear title. If they buy a property, they do own it, they can rent it and live in it, but they can never refinance it or get a mortgage on it because they can't get title insurance. That means they can never sell it because the new buyer can't get a mortgage. That's the way some tax foreclosures laws have been written.

There are ways to clear title by filing a lawsuit and going to court. It's called a quiet title action. It's complicated, but it can be done.

Just be careful. Before you buy any property, anywhere, for any price, make sure that you're getting clear title and can get title insurance.

get the property. In others, you have to wait a year to see if the original owner pays it off (this is called right of redemption), which in some areas is two years. In other areas, you can't get clear title.

Instead of wondering or worrying about it, make a couple of phone calls. Your job as a real estate investor is to stay focused on helping people and making money. While you can spend a lot of time studying the technicalities and terminology involved, and the differences in every city's and state's ever-changing laws, you need to focus on the end result. Call a local title lawyer and ask, "Do I get the property? Can I get title insurance?" It's important to determine if you can make some money on the deal.

Remember, almost all loans and liens are negotiable. If you never ask for a discount, you'll never get one. So before you pay off any loan or lien, ask for a discount. Any time you ask a question, there are only three responses you can get: yes, no, or maybe. So ask, ask, ask.

In major cities, tax sales have become highly competitive. A lot of investors bid on these properties. My strategy is this: Go to small towns, out in the middle of nowhere. There are real opportunities in small towns, away from the competition.

Foreclosure Sales

When you go to a foreclosure sale, who else is there? Buyers, sellers, and people with money. Network and get to know these people. They buy deals, they sell deals, and they can pass deals on. You might even find a deal at the sale.

Let me tell you a secret about foreclosures. When you go to the courthouse, you'll see 100 people on the downtown courthouse steps. The same 5 or 10 people are always buying the properties, like a little insider club (which you should get into—there's always room for one more).

Let's say you looked at a house that appeared to be a good deal. You think it's worth $200,000. It's being foreclosed on, and somebody bids $190,000 on it. You'll find out it's usually the bank who bids that high because they lent $190,000. Everyone else at the foreclosure sale will probably shrug their shoulders, get upset, and go home.

When you are outbid, never quit, and never get upset. Instead, approach the buyers and ask what they're going to do with the property. As in the example above, call the bank who bought it. The bankers might say, "We lent $190,000 on the property, but now we've got to dump it. Make an offer." So you offer $110,000. Maybe they take it. Maybe they don't.

In another example, an investor might buy a property at a tax sale to wholesale it. That investor could actually wholesale it to you, so contact the buyer and ask. Then find out what else this investor wants to buy and go find it. That person could become your new best client.

You're always networking, always finding buyers. Most great deals come from networking—someone you met at a foreclosure, someone you met at a real estate meeting, a friend took you to lunch. If you don't want to do this part of the business, find someone who does.

DAY 4   Action Plan

It's Up to You to Make It Happen!

✔ Go to the courthouse, find the registrar of deeds, and have the employees show you how to do a title search. I'm not recommending that you do these searches consistently. That activity won't make you any money. But become familiar with them and the process they employ.

✔ Who helped you at the courthouse? Keep in contact with them, because they could give you leads.

✔ Go to a foreclosure sale. Meet people. Get names and numbers.

✔ Find out who's buying. These are people with money. They could become your money sources. List them here.

Buyer _____   Phone number _____

Buyer _____   Phone number _____

Buyer _____   Phone number _____

Buyer _____   Phone number _____

Buyer _____   Phone number _____

Ask what the buyers will do with the properties, and take notes here. Maybe they'll sell their properties to you in the future.

_____

_____

_____

_____

What other types of properties are these potential future buyers looking for?
List them here.

_____

_____

_____

_____

Foreclosures, Part 2

Although you can go to the court to find foreclosure deals, why not go directly to the source? Instead of waiting for foreclosure sales, you can buy foreclosed property from the finance companies themselves.

Finance Companies

Today, you'll call finance companies. Get out your Yellow Pages, and look up Mortgage Finance Companies. These are the B- and C-grade mortgage finance companies. They make higher-risk loans, with lower loan-to-values. They have names that include the words "Associates," "Beneficial," "Commercial Credit," to name a few.

Call the phone numbers, and ask for the managers. Tell them you're looking for deals in real estate. Ask if they have any property now or if there are any properties they will soon be repossessing.

These companies make riskier loans than banks and mortgage companies. People they lend to don't have perfect credit, so often the companies end up taking a lot of property back. Sometimes, the property returns are handled locally, sometimes regionally, and sometimes nationally.

Ask these lenders to send you a list of all the properties they're taking back. If you've contacted a company that handles its repossessions nationally, some properties will be in your state, while some will be in other states.

Most investors toss out the information regarding property in other states. Not you! Use the same analysis on those out-of-state properties as you would for local ones, and when you find a deal, call the local real estate association, get on the Internet, find the I Buy Houses ads in that area. Make a couple of phone calls to source a local buyer for the deal you've found.

I've wholesaled two properties that way in other states. I never even saw the properties. I used the same system: Do the analysis, put the property under contract, and wholesale it to a local investor.

Foreclosure Sales

If you're going to a foreclosure sale to buy a property, you'll need cash and a letter of credit. If the government or the bank is foreclosing and they're selling the property at the courthouse or at a foreclosure sale, once you put a contract in, you generally have from 0 to 10 days to deliver cash.

If you don't have a lot of money, find a partner with good credit or a lot of cash, or go to a hard moneylender. (You'll have homework on Day 25 to find hard moneylenders and other people with cash.) Another way to find people with money is to notice who is buying property at the foreclosure sale. They have cash or credit, so get to know them.

> Why would people at a foreclosure sale want to talk to you? Because you can help them. Find out what they want. If they're buying property, find out what they're looking for, so down the road, if you locate property that fits their criteria, you can sell it to them.

It All Comes Down to Money

Let's cut to the chase. You can buy a property through owner's terms, lease option, or wholesaling, all without using your own money or credit. But the person who has the most cash will get the best deals. It's as simple as that.

If you approach sellers and tell them you can meet owner's terms or pay them off in six months to a year, or that you have partners who can, they might sign a contract with you—or not. But if someone walks up and says, "I'll pay you cash for your property. I can close tomorrow," who's going to get the better deal?

Cash is king. So if you don't have it, find somebody who does. Get access to it through a partner, an associate, or a hard moneylender. I recommend you find all three. When you come across that great deal, you'll want to be able to close quickly.

Caveat

Although foreclosure sales work and many of my students make a lot of money finding deals through them, I generally don't like them for three reasons: They're very competitive, you need a lot of cash, and you can't inspect the property. I know plenty of other ways to find deals. But some people love to work foreclosures, and there certainly are deals to be found.

DAY 5   Action Plan

It's Up to You to Make It Happen!

✔ Today, call eight to nine finance companies. Do they have any property, or will they soon be repossessing any property that you could buy?

Company _____ Phone number _____

Property description _____

Company _____ Phone number _____

Property description _____

Company _____ Phone number _____

Property description _____

Company _____ Phone number _____

Property description _____

Company _____ Phone number _____

Property description _____

Company _____ Phone number _____

Property description _____

Company _____ Phone number _____

Property description _____

Company _____ Phone number _____

Property description _____

Friday Check-In

Day 6 could land in the first week, second week, or even third week after you start your business, depending on the pace at which you're going. But by now, you've been doing real estate for five days. You're still looking for deals, but there's something important to take care of. Whatever day this comes out on for you, you've got to do the activities on what I call your Special Friday.

Special Friday

You can pick a day other than Friday—but you've got to do this once a week. There's no option. Every Friday, spend 30 to 40 minutes to step back and carefully examine your entire business.

That means review both your business and household budgets. Be aware of what's coming in and what's going out every week. Of course, if you're just getting started, you may have lots of money going out and none coming in—yet. But still

> Doing this addresses the number one killer of businesses: lack of cash flow. A lot of businesses make money but don't have the proper cash flow to keep it going. Without good cash flow, they don't have a cushion or the capital to weather a few poor-income weeks in their business. All of a sudden, a good business can be out of business. Because of this, I set aside time every Friday and I look at the cash-flow statement for my business.

track it. If you're not able to, hire a bookkeeper to do it, because you need a weekly statement of what's coming into and going out of your business.

You may shy away from looking at your financial statement every week because it could be so depressing. But I think one of the best motivators is desperation. It gets you moving and thinking. Look at financial statements for both your personal budget and your real estate business, and you'll know where your finances stand.

Tracking Your Time

Let's say you have a real estate business, and you hire someone to operate it for $50,000 a year. After he's worked for two months, you check on his progress and ask, "What have you been doing?"

"I don't know," he says.

"I've paid you."

"Yeah, I know. I've cashed the checks."

> I'm trained as an attorney. I worked for a law firm for one summer. That's as much as I could take. But I did learn something extremely interesting from attorneys: the importance of tracking your time. When you work for a law firm, the partners make you track your time in seven-minute increments. They want to know what you've been doing, and that's how they bill the clients. They bill their phone calls in seven-second increments. They know what everyone is doing and where the money is coming from.

He's been busy talking on the phone with his friends and playing games on the computer, but he hasn't been making any money. What would you do with that employee? You'd put him on notice. Well, if you're accomplishing nothing with the time you're spending, you'll have to put yourself on notice, too! I certainly hope you're tracking your time, so that you know what's actually getting done.

Tracking your time is good business. From now on, track your time, track what's making you money, and track your cash flow. Do this every Friday. How can you improve and become more efficient if you don't know what you're doing, how you're spending your time, or whether you're making any money? Scrutinize your own use of time just as you would an employee's.

Track your time every day and total it every Friday. It's a discipline. You have to do it. Fill out your checklist (see the Action Plan at the end of this chapter for a copy). Looking back, you'll be amazed at how you spend your time. Once, I spent 30 minutes looking for paper clips! I've actually spent an hour looking for a CD. You might spend time doing the laundry, watching TV, folding paper—doing anything but work. You can be extremely busy without being productive. So focus on your productive time—time that will help you find sellers, buyers, and money—time that makes deals happen.

The most successful real estate investors in the country are probably spending up to 15 hours a week doing productive activity. Please don't get me wrong. They're busy 40 hours a week, but how much of that is really productive time? A

What's the real reason you should get into real estate investing? Consider what an hour is worth when you are spending time with your family and friends, tending to spiritual pursuits, and doing other things you really enjoy. These hours are priceless. Every hour you spend working, you can't spend doing what's really important to you.

That's why you need to make a lot of money during the time you're working. You want to weigh the time you spend working against the cost of not doing what you really want to be doing. This issue is not about the cost of what you *are* doing, but about the cost of what you're *not* doing. That's what's important. Make it count. Make your money in a fewer number of hours, and free up time for the rest of your living.

fraction of it, and I'm referring to people making from $100,000 to $400,000 a year. So if you spend 15 to 20 hours a week focused and productive, guess how much money you may be able to make over time? A large number could be very realistic.

A study about salespeople concluded that in the 1920s, the average salesperson spent 11 to 15 hours a week doing productive sales activities. In the year 2000, after all the sales training, new sales techniques and developments have been put in place, guess how much time the best sales people spent a week in productive sales activities? About the same amount. Can you imagine if those people spent 20 hours a week productively?

What can we conclude from this? First, don't feel bad if you're not super-productive. You're probably still above average. Second, try to be a little bit more productive, and you'll be head and shoulders above the rest. Imagine if you could spend just five more hours a week on productive activity, how much bigger and better your business would be. In addition to that, as you make money, you'll hire others to perform more of these activities. You'll leverage your time.

Top Five Priorities

One of the most helpful tools I've used is this: Every morning, I spend the first 15 minutes making a list of my top five priorities to accomplish that day. I highly recommend you do that, too. Most people wake up, hit the ground running, and react to what comes their way. The phone rings, they run around town and take care of people, and all of a sudden, the day's gone and they haven't accomplished anything they wanted to.

So every morning, or the night before, write down the top five definite things you want to accomplish. Of course, include in that list these Action Plans for success: go to foreclosure sale, call real estate agents—whatever your task is for that day.

Take a few minutes, plan your day, put your priorities in writing, and make sure you get those five things done. You can use a PDA, planner, pad of paper—whatever system works for you. The key is to make sure you get these five priorities done.

Financial Housecleaning

On Day 6, start filling out your productivity chart. Be diligent. Make sure you get those budgets done. Every Friday, demand from yourself and your bookkeeper to know what the business's cash flow is—what's coming in and what's going out.

Every month and every quarter, do a financial statement; review it carefully. By doing this, you'll be set at the end of the year instead of scrambling. Once you get into real estate, your financial situation should be much better after two years. I hope you'll be making more money, bringing in more cash, and building more net worth through your real estate equity. Take a snapshot now and then regularly down the road. Keep comparing the numbers.

Day 6   Action Plan

It's Up to You to Make It Happen!

✔ Check your weekly financial statement for both your real estate business and your personal budget.

✔ Total the time you spent on each activity this week, and fill in the rest of the chart below.

Productivity Chart

Activity	Time Spent	Profitable?	Enjoyable?	Am I good at it?	Can someone else do it?
Called real estate agents	30 minutes	0			
Called mortgage brokers		0			
Went to foreclosure sale	one hour	0			
Driving for dollars	two hours	0			
Bookkeeping	four hours	0	0	0	after a while

Under the "Profitable" heading, enter your actual earnings; the first month might have all zeros, but after six months to a year, you'll see profits.

Looking through the Newspaper

The basis of real estate investors' success lies in finding good deals rather than ordinary ones. You don't even need to get dressed up to find good deals. Just grab a cup of coffee and scour the newspaper.

Which newspaper? Although you can look in your city's major newspaper, the local, regional newspapers are even better. They're much less expensive to advertise in. You're looking for motivated sellers, and they're looking to save money, so they often choose these papers to advertise in. You'll get a lot more for your time by combing through local papers. Still, spend a few hours a week looking through the major newspaper, too.

Many great deals are there, section after section, ready to be found—by you! Remember, you're looking for a motivated seller. Sometimes, the ads will tell you directly, saying, "Motivated seller," "Must sell," or "Must liquidate." Mostly, you'll infer the motivation by combing the following sections.

What to Look For in the Newspaper

For Sale by Owner Ads

If people try to sell their properties and don't want to get a Realtor involved, they have strong motivation to sell. Maybe they don't want to pay a real estate agent's commission, or they don't have time to get an agent. These ads can lead to finding a good deal quickly, because you can negotiate directly with the decision maker.

Lease with Option to Buy Ads

These involve real estate investors doing lease options. They may be motivated. They may be willing to do owner's terms. It's definitely worthwhile to find the other players in the market who are doing lease options.

When you're calling For Sale by Owner and Lease Option ads, here are the three questions you should ask. (1) Are they motivated sellers? (2) Are they buyers? (3) Do they have any money? By probing for answers to these three questions, you've tripled your rate of success with every call.

For Rent Ads

For Rent ads are among my favorites to call on. I'm not saying this is the only way or the best way to find deals, but in every major city where my students have said no deals exist, I can call from 50 to 100 For Rent ads and find deals.

Who's on the other end of a For Rent ad? Either a landlord or property manager. The property must be empty because they're running a For Rent ad. Likely, the tenants left it in poor condition, and they aren't collecting rent on it. They just may be motivated.

Additionally, if they're landlords, they probably bought the property years ago, paying half of what it's worth now. Even though they've heard its value has increased, in their mind, it's still worth what they paid for it. Therefore, they might be willing to sell it for less than current market value.

Let's say a house worth $150,000, and the rent is $1,000 a month. Does that mean the landlord is making $1,000 a month? No. He's spending a lot of time and effort to take care of the property. He's managing it, or paying a manager. He's spending a lot of money on repairs. Currently, it's empty. So run the numbers, and ask the following questions:

- How long has it been empty?
- How much have you spent on repairs in the last two or three years?
- How much time do you spend going back and forth?
- How much time do you spend worrying about it?
- How much time do you spend trying to rent it?
- How much time do you spend with paperwork and phone calls?
- Are you free? Can you travel?
- What is your hour worth?

Then run the numbers with the landlord. He's not collecting $1,000 a month because it's been empty two months this year, so he's only collecting $833 a month. He has all of these expenses and headaches. Point out, for example, that in the last three years, he spent $3,000 fixing the property, painting it, replacing carpets, and so on. That's $250 a month. With repairs and vacancies, he's really only making between $500 and $600 a month.

On almost any rental property, you can take 30 percent to 40 percent off the top for vacancy, management, and repair expenses. That's something most investing books and seminars never tell you. You may be an exception. You may have a rental property that's been full all year and has had no repairs. If so, you're very lucky. Over a 5 to 10-year period, you'll still have to fix things, paint, replace carpet, or replace the roof and hot water heater. Managing property takes thousands and thousands of dollars.

After you point out that he's really only making a fraction of what he assumed, he could be motivated to let you take over the property, so that he can get out of the headache business, get out of the repair business, get out of the tenant business. Then he'd be free to travel and pursue his hobbies. Talk with him about doing a lease option or selling the property. Make a quick profit and move on.

Most people call 20 For Rent ads and only reach one or two people. They leave a bunch of voicemails and no one calls them back. After that, they quit.

I'm willing to call at least 100 For Rent ads. Out of 100 ads, I usually get through to about eight people. I leave voicemails with the rest, and between four and eight people call me back. So I'm lucky to get a 10 percent to 15 percent response rate.

Most people lose interest and quit too quickly. One of my deals in South Florida resulted from making 150 calls on For Rent ads. I only got a hold of 15 people, with callbacks and leaving messages. But of the 15 people, I connected with one landlord who had two deals and had only closed on one of them. I wholesaled his condominium and made $28,000. Do the math: $28,000 divided by 150 calls equals $187 per call.

The way I look at business is this: I don't care that I called 150 people and most people didn't call me back. I look at what I make per phone call. Now that's just to find the deal. Then I had to put it under contract and find a buyer, so there's more work involved than the initial round of calls. And deals do fall through occasionally; nothing works out perfectly.

But consider this: Would you make a call knowing you'd earn $187 to make it? Let's say you're not very skilled yet, and you only average $50 a call. Would you still be interested in making a call to earn $50? Do you currently make $50 for every phone call you make? Of all my students tracking calls on For Rent ads, the least successful one I've heard of is making $30 a call—and he didn't follow my system. Still, that's not bad. Unfortunately, most people will make a few calls, get no response, decide this doesn't work, and quit.

Consider this: If I've made 149 calls and still haven't found a deal but have confidence that I can make an average of $187 a call, I'll make another one (or whatever the call ratio is). The point is this: Calling is worth your time and effort. Track the number of calls you make, the number of responses you get, and the amount of money you make. I promise, if you call For Rent ads in the next year, you'll find deals.

What are the two things landlords and property managers hate about their property? (1) Collecting rent, (2) Making repairs. If tenants always paid their rent on time and there were no repairs, no one would complain about rental property. So when you talk to landlords, keep in mind you're here to fix problems. Tell them, "I have a program. I need to see whether you're qualified—you might or might not be. This program will get you out of the repair business and make sure you get your rent on time, all the time. Would you be interested? Please call." (Leave your name and phone number.)

Most beginners in real estate investing call with an apologetic attitude. They want something the owner has and aren't sure they'll be able to get it. So using the script on the previous page, you're posturing. You're telling them you have something they might not be able to get. You have to see if they're qualified, because you have the goods: the information, the knowledge, and the program.

For Sale through Real Estate Agents

Usually, if a house is listed by a real estate agent, the sellers are not highly motivated. The real estate agent has done an appraisal and run comparable sales, advising the seller to list the property for what it's worth—or even more. However, these agents might *know* of some motivated sellers. And remember, you're always building your team of experts.

Real estate brokers are valuable team members for several reasons:

- They know the market.
- They can help you assess what properties are worth.
- They can help you find a buyer and sell a property.

Probate, Estate Sales, Divorces, Bankruptcy, Foreclosures, and Auction Announcements

You can specialize in one or two of these areas. Taking ethical shortcuts, I suggest you find out who works in these areas at the courthouse and take them to lunch. Tell them you're looking for deals in real estate and that you'll pay them a finder's fee. The transactions become public record, but you still must respect client confidentiality.

Read announcements about upcoming auctions and court actions. Then attend them.

- You might find an incredible deal.
- You'll meet buyers who have cash.

Talk to everyone there, get contact information, and use it to build your buyer database.

Obituaries

If an obituary is in the newspaper, what does that mean to you? The deceased usually leaves behind real estate, furniture, cars, and family members who live all over the country. You could be doing the relatives a service by writing or calling them and saying, "I am so sorry to hear about your loss, but if you have any property you want to dispose of quickly, I can help. I might be interested in taking it over." In a lot of cases, people say, "We don't want to mess with this house. The children and cousins have moved across the country. Just take the house; you're doing us a favor. Yes, we know we're selling way below what it is worth, but we don't have time to deal with it. There are too many memories there. Just take it."

Investment Property Ads

Investment Property ads are for properties being sold by investors and landlords. They may not know enough about investing or analyzing or managing property. They may be losing money on their properties or deciding to retire. Find out their situations; these sellers could be highly motivated.

After a rich man in Nashville passed away, Bill, a friend of mine, read the obituary in the newspaper and called the widow. She had just inherited 14 apartment buildings and 20 small houses—property she didn't want to deal with. She was happy to sell them to my friend for 50 cents on the dollar. She offered owner's terms and made a lot of money.

He also asked her the magic question: *"Do you have anything else you'd like to sell?"* She took him out back to the barn, where she showed him 20 collector cars her husband had acquired. He bought them all for $50,000, and sold one of the 20 for that exact amount. The proceeds from the other 19 were pure cream on top.

The lesson is this: Be aware, look in the paper, and make that phone call. Why did Bill find all those deals and make all that money, while I didn't? Because he picked up the phone and asked. I wished real estate was a bit more complicated than that, but it's really not.

> Most of my deals are done with other investors. They understand investing. They understand that I've got to buy a deal; they know I understand they need to make a little money. They won't try to sell property for full price to another investor. Most real estate investors are good people, and you'll want to get to know them.

Why Work with Other Investors?

Pay special attention to I Buy Houses ads, Lease with the Option to Buy ads, For Rent ads, and Investment Property ads. They'll lead you to other investors. Think of other investors not as the competition, but as your partners. Remember, you're always building your three lists: sellers, buyers, and sources of money. Investors are all three.

1. *They're sellers.* They may find deals they don't want (a deal may be in an area they're not interested in, or they may not have enough money at the time). You want to be on their list of people to call when they do have a deal.

2. *They're buyers.* Meet them, talk to them, so that when you find a deal, you can call them. They may buy it.

3. *They're sources of money.* They may be interested in a joint venture or in lending money to help you close a deal.

Sellers Are Buyers in Disguise

Even if an Investment Property ad advertises property for *sale*, it may also be alerting you to people interested in *buying* property. Usually, they're running the ad because they're going to buy another deal, and they want to sell an old deal to make money or clear up their credit to buy the new one. Once again, Investment Property ads are sources of buyers, sellers, and people with money. Call them.

Finding Investors to Take to Lunch

Remember that one of your Action Plan items is to take investors to lunch. How do you find these investors? Besides tapping your local real estate association, use ads as another source of investors. Call the advertisers, tell them you're starting out in real estate and want to learn more. Of course, ask them if they have time to talk. Be respectful; chances are they're busy people. If you leave a voicemail message, make sure you leave a message that will compel them to call you back. You can leave your name and phone number, but if they don't even know who you are, they probably won't call back. Instead, think of something they're interested in, and connect to that. For example, you might have property they'd be interested in buying, or perhaps you have a friend in common. (See "Leaving Phone Messages" in Day 9 for more ideas.)

Sending Letters

One of my students concentrates his business on writing letters to family members grieving after a death. He finds names from obituaries in the newspaper. It works. He's helping people sell things quickly and settle the estate. Families are very appreciative that someone is willing to come and take it all: houses, cars, and furniture. You too can provide this service.

If you're making calls or sending letters based on obituaries, please be very sensitive. Remember, you're dealing with people who have just experienced a death. My student's letter reads: "I understand you've just had a loss in the family. If there is any real estate that you would like to sell, I may be able to buy it quickly. Please call me."

Expect realistic responses. If you send out the best letter in the world, the average response rate to direct mail is 1 percent to 2 percent. Even if you're offering gold bricks, unlimited wealth, weight loss, or free money, you'll still only get a 1 percent to 2 percent response rate. You're playing a numbers game. Most people aren't willing to send the volume of letters that is required to get the needed response rate. I highly recommend that you spend a few extra minutes to double your response rate by doing a few simple things:

1. Hand write the address, then you'll get more people to open the envelope.

2. Include the following message in bold print on the envelope: "We May Have Money for You." If you received an envelope that said that, would you open it and read the letter? Most likely. A compelling message increases your success rate.

3. Make sure the first line of your letter is written in a forceful way.

To triple or quadruple your response rate, follow your letter with a phone call. At the bottom of the letter, write "Please expect a phone call." When you call and someone asks who you are and why you're calling, you can say, "They're expecting my call." Or you can say, "It's personal." Or even, "It's a legal matter." Check with your attorney and do only what you feel is legal, ethical, and honest.

When people don't call back, leave a polite message every day until they do. If you need to talk to someone, instead of wondering or worrying, pick up the phone and dial 7 to 10 numbers. Think from the other person's point of view; try to return everyone's phone call within one business day. If you want to be in the top 10 percent of whatever business you're in, just calling people back makes a huge difference.

Where Are the Deals?

There are deals in every type of neighborhood, but you're more likely to find a deal in a neighborhood that's in transition, a neighborhood that's being fixed up. A low-to-moderate income neighborhood usually has more deals than the brand-new, high-end subdivision (although some deals can be found in those areas, too).

Remember, you don't have to live in or love the neighborhood to make money. You're focused on helping people and then making a profit. If you do one deal in an area where you're not comfortable, you'll quickly feel more at ease. Once you get past your first few deals, you'll realize that a deal is a deal, no matter where it is.

Learning the Real Estate Market

Go through the newspaper once or twice a week. In addition to finding buyers and sellers, you'll find a lot of market information. Do you know people who read the sports section in the newspaper every day? After a month or two, they can tell you the players, how much they weigh, where they went to school, and their statistics.

What would happen if those people spent that much time looking at the real estate section? Within a month, you can learn the prices of houses in different areas, what the rents are, who the Realtors are, what the supplies and activities are. You can learn all this in the real estate section. That's how you learn the market.

If you're serious about real estate investing, make a habit of looking through the newspaper. Spend an hour, or more, looking through the Sunday real estate section for at least the next 90 days. Also make it a habit to look through the real estate section on at least one other day of the week, usually a Wednesday or Thursday. But always look on Sunday.

Besides having great information about the market (interest rates, players, sellers, and buyers), the newspaper has helpful articles about mortgages, mortgage rates, trends in real estate, and new developments. If you read the newspaper regularly, you'll become an expert on your local real estate market. Many newspapers are also available on the Internet, so if you're interested in another city or area, get online and start reading its real estate section.

Commit to educating yourself about your real estate market—the different areas and prices—so you'll recognize the deals.

DAY 7   Action Plan

It's Up to You to Make It Happen!

✔ Today, you're looking for *potentially* motivated sellers who may be prospects. Circle the following ads in your newspaper: For Sale by Owner ads, Lease with Option to Buy ads, For Rent ads, For Sale ads, Make Offer, Must Sell, I Buy Houses ads, court announcements, obituaries, and Investment Property ads. Which newspapers do you use? You should also read local shoppers' news, big city papers, and legal newspapers.

List the newspapers you scoured today.

_____

Names and contact information of investors you found in the paper:

_____   _____

_____   _____

_____   _____

_____   _____

_____   _____

What did you learn about the real estate market from the newspaper?

_____

_____

_____

List active real estate agents.

_____   _____

_____   _____

_____   _____

List the potentially motivated sellers you found, with their contact information. Tomorrow, you'll make these phone calls.

_____   _____

_____   _____

_____   _____

_____   _____

_____   _____

_____   _____

_____   _____

_____   _____

_____   _____

_____   _____

_____   _____

_____   _____

_____   _____

_____   _____

_____   _____

_____   _____

Making Phone Calls, Part 1

Most people don't like to make phone calls. They associate it with the cold calls telemarketers make to sell something people probably don't even want. But in real estate, you're calling people who *want* to sell something. Don't fret about making the call; by placing the ad, the prospective seller has invited you to pick up the phone.

If you just absolutely can't stand making phone calls, however, then find someone who is very outgoing, talks a lot, and loves chatting. You can write a script and pay the right people to make the calls for you. The beauty of business is finding ways to leverage your time. There are only so many calls you can make and only so many properties you can look at, so why not have others doing it for you? I like to pay people a finder's fee or commission. If they find a prospect, I pay them a little bit. If the prospect becomes a full-fledged deal and we close on a good-sized property, I pay them a huge commission. That's highly motivating!

I think the best way to make phone calls is to be completely honest, which can actually be disarming. Throughout this book, you'll learn a lot of negotiation and persuasion techniques. In fact, people pay thousands of dollars for books, seminars, and courses to learn the principles contained in this material. Follow these ideas, and you'll get similar value and results. So let's get started.

Phone Calling 101

Block Time

First, block time out in your schedule to focus on making phone calls. *Don't try to sandwich calls between all the other things you're doing that day.* Make calling a priority. On this day, Day 8, take 90 to 120 minutes to make phone calls. Turn everything else off, shut the door, and focus on just making phone calls.

Number of Calls

How many phone calls can you make in an hour? A professional telemarketer can make between 30 to 50, so you can probably make at least 20 to 30. At least, set that as your goal, and be sure to track the ones you make.

Gather Information

From your very first call, all you want to do is gather information. That is initially your only mission: to gather information.

Techniques for Success on the Phone

As a beginning real estate investor calling people for the first time, you're nervous and excited. The task seems difficult. You're unsure what to say. So here's how most novice phone conversations go: "Hi. My name is _____. I'm a real estate investor. I don't know what I'm doing, but maybe you've got something for sale . . . and are you motivated?" Feeling nervous, they talk too much and don't have the presence of mind even to listen to answers.

Don't fall into the traps that hurt so many novices. To succeed on the phone, use these techniques:

✔ First, *relax*. Take a few deep breaths and focus.

✔ Second, remember that the less you care, the more money you'll make. So *don't care*; have fun.

✔ Third, use posturing to *portray yourself as a busy real estate professional.* That's the attitude you must have, whether you're just beginning or have been working for 10 years.

✔ Fourth, when I call about real estate, the *last word I mention is real estate.* I'm genuinely interested in the people I'm talking with so I ask about what they do, where they live, etc. I let them ask why I called. Then, the real estate becomes a "by the way" aside rather than the focus of the call.

✔ Fifth, *build rapport*, making them feel comfortable with you and you with them. Studies show that people like to do business with people they like.

✔ Sixth, *match their style.* I've learned from martial arts that if you want to win a fight or any kind of conflict, use whatever energy your opponents use against them. Don't use *your* energy; use *theirs.* For example, if you call someone and say, "Hi, my name's _____ and I'm calling about your real estate," and he's loud and abrupt, then match his style and speak loudly and quickly, getting right to the point.

Alternatively, if you call someone who's quiet and peaceful on the phone and speaks with a low voice, match this style with a quiet, peaceful demeanor and low voice.

And for Openers

Have you ever received a sales call when you're about to sit down to dinner? What do you do? You get upset and try to get the caller off the phone any way you can. Don't fall victim to this!

Here's one of the best ways to make calls, because it's extremely honest as well as effective: Call and say, "Hi. My name is _____. I know you don't

I suggest that you play with this style of calling and become comfortable with it until you find your own style. When I respond to a For Rent ad and someone picks up the phone, I say, "Hi. My name's Robert. What's your name?" Then I ask, "Where do you live?" He usually gives me the name of the neighborhood. Then I ask, "How long have you lived there?" I might ask where he works and how long he's been there. At this point, some people say, "Hey, wait a minute! Why are you calling? Who are you?" And I'll say, "Oh, by the way, I'm calling on a For Rent ad." I never bring it up first. I want to build rapport first.

The problem with most beginning investors is that *they care way too much* about the real estate and getting the call done. In my experience, that approach will hurt you. So, care less. Have fun. And be genuinely interested in the people you're calling.

To reduce my nervousness and tension while I'm on the phone, I usually do something else while I make the calls, such as skim a book or magazine. Maybe you'd like surf the Internet. That will make you care a little bit less and make calling a little more pleasant. If you worry too much about doing anything, it can become nervewracking.

know me, and I know you probably don't like getting phone calls like this." Then be silent for a minute. You've just addressed exactly what they're thinking. This will disarm the person you're talking to. Then say right up front, "Look, I'm a beginning real estate investor, and I'm not very good at this. I don't really know what I'm doing." Pause again. Then say, "However, I'm trying to find a few good deals and was wondering if you would answer a few questions. I might not even ask them right."

This honest, up-front approach disarms people, makes them feel comfortable, and gets good results. There's nothing wrong with telling people you're new at real estate investing, and don't know what you're doing. But, gee, you're trying. And if you're relaxed and having fun, the people you're calling will relax and have fun. Alternatively, if you're uptight and nervous, the people you're calling will be uptight and nervous. So give what you want to get.

If you're calling on a foreclosure, keep in mind that the people involved may be under pressure, in denial, and getting a lot of calls. In that situation, say, "I know you're getting a lot of calls, and a lot of letters, and people are coming after you. I don't want anything, relax. How are you feeling?" Let them talk. Ask if they're confused about the process, if they have any questions, or if there's any way you can help.

Here are three key questions you want to get answered for any property you're calling about. If you're calling on a For Sale ad ask

1. Why are you selling?
2. Why are you selling?
3. Why are you selling?

The reason for such repetition is that you have to find out if they're actually motivated to sell.

The first time you ask, most people won't tell you the real reason they're selling their property. You have find out what the real problem is—the *serious* motivation behind selling the property. Usually, you have to ask "why are you selling?" several times to uncover the true reason. And even then, they might not have a reason. That's also important to know, because you're looking for motivated sellers. You're looking for people who are willing to sell their properties for 15 percent to 30 percent below market value. If they're not motivated, they're not going to sell at a discount. So if they answer, "We just want to sell our house; we have plenty of time; there's no rush; the real estate agent told us it's worth $1 million and we want to get that for it; we have no particular reason for selling." If that's the truth, those sellers clearly aren't motivated to sell at the below-market price you're looking for. But they may also tell you, "We have to move out of state quickly. I've got a new job and we have to be in our new location within a month." In this case, they're likely highly motivated to sell.

Often, people say they have to sell the house because they need the money. Most real estate investors stop right there, but you won't make that mistake. You'll keep asking questions. Ask, "What do you need the money for?" If they say they have to pay off some debt, ask how much the debt is. I suggest you strive to uncover the exact numerical reason why they're selling their property.

Are you surprised that people actually reveal these details on a first phone call? That's why trust-building telephone techniques are so important. You have

I like to say I'm a real estate doctor because my focus is to help people. I tell them I'm here to help them solve their problem if they have one. If they don't have a problem, I offer to help them sell their house anyway. So if they're not motivated and they want to sell their house, I may refer them to a real estate agent or give them an idea how to market their property. My number one priority is helping people. If they don't have a problem, I can't help them.

to build rapport. In addition to asking questions, be upfront and honest about what you're doing. This is the best way to disarm people and make them feel comfortable. Tell them you're a real estate investor who's looking to buy property at below market and you're here to help.

Sometimes, people you call won't talk to you. They may become upset and hang up. At some point, most investors quit and move on, but you won't. Your backup plan is to shoot out a low offer, say 60 percent of the asking price. If the real estate agent won't call you back or the person on the phone won't communicate with you, shoot out another low offer. Keep in mind that this entire process is designed to find motivated sellers.

So if the sellers have their house for sale at an asking price of $600,000, shoot them a low offer at $359,817. Learn how to make risk-free offers. Your offer might include the following terms: 75 days to close and a statement saying, "This contract is contingent upon buyer's inspection and approval before closing," or "This contract is contingent upon finding favorable financing."

Contingency Clause

If you were buying a house for yourself, your contract would most likely have a contingency clause stating something like this: "This contract is contingent upon getting a good mortgage from a lender." If you couldn't obtain funding from the

Remember, even though I've been in real estate for over 12 years and teach how to make phone calls, I almost never do it perfectly myself. I usually leave something out. After I hang up, I remember something I should have asked. Know that feeling? Of course, you can always call the person back. Calling a second time often proves to be much easier.

Please understand that this is not a test. You don't have to make each call perfectly. You can miss half the questions and do half of the things wrong, but just by making the call—if you make enough of them—you'll make something happen.

bank or mortgage company, or privately, you wouldn't have to buy the house, because you included the contingency clause in your contract.

What's your risk in sending out that contract? None. What's your risk in *not* sending that offer out? You could lose a potential deal. You never know. You might also include a line in the contract that says, "This offer is only good for one business day" or "This offer is only good for 48 hours from receipt." Or put a date on which the offer will expire. Don't make an open-ended offer that doesn't specify a time to reply; if you give people an unlimited time in which to do something, they'll probably never do it. If you give them a week, they'll probably respond on the seventh or eighth day. So when you're making offers, don't allow too much time to reply.

To build a greater sense of immediacy, include a cover letter that states you're making offers on a lot of other properties. Restate the time frame you stipulated on the contract: "This offer is only good for 48 hours from receipt," for example. "It expires this Friday at midnight, so please respond." Then, include your phone number. Close the letter with a note that you will be calling. Then follow through. Take the time to make one more phone call.

Property Analysis Worksheet

When you're calling in response to an ad you found in the newspaper on Day 7, ask the person who answers (and likely placed the ads) the following questions:

- Seller's name _____
- Address of the property _____
- Phone number _____
- Why are you selling? _____
- How long have you been trying to sell the property? _____
- What did you buy the property for? _____

(If the person says, "I'm not going to tell you that, it's personal," respond with, "That's fine, it's public record, I'll just look it up. It doesn't matter to me." Remember, you don't care that much. It's just business.)

- What is the mortgage? _____

(Again, if the person doesn't want to tell you, be easygoing about it and say it doesn't matter to you; it's public record, you'll just look it up.)

- Do you own the property that's for sale? Yes or No

(Only negotiate with the decision maker. You may be talking to someone for a while and discover he's not the owner but the third cousin who just happened to pick up the phone. He's not the person you want to talk to or negotiate with; he can't make a decision.)

- Who holds title to the property? _____

(If the bank took back the property last week but the people are still living in it, then talk to the bank's representative. The bank holds title and owns the property.)

- What is the property worth? _____
- How did you come up with that number? _____

(Be sure they are comparing apples to apples and oranges to oranges. They may think their house is worth the same as one that sold down the street. But if the one down the street is newer or bigger, they've got the wrong price in mind. If all the houses on the street are about the same, the price quote may be on target.)

■ What repairs are needed? How much would they cost? _____

_____

_____

(Once a deal progresses, be sure to verify these expenses. Send out a contractor to inspect the house. But in the preliminary stages, when you're finding out whether it's a deal worth pursuing, keep in mind that most sellers do know what repairs are needed and how much they'll cost. So ask them. If they say no repairs are needed, use my system to go from top to bottom. Visualize the house, start at the top, and go down.) How's the roof? How's the ceiling? Walls? Bedrooms? Bathrooms? Kitchen? Floor? Stairs? Foundation? Windows? Yard?

■ How soon do you have to sell the house? _____

(If they say they're in no rush—they've got two years—they're not motivated. If, on the other hand, they say they've got to sell it within 20 days or the bank will take it back, you've found a motivated seller.)

■ How old is the house? _____

■ If mortgage payments are in arrears, by how much? _____

■ How much are the taxes on it? _____

■ What is the insurance coverage on it?_____

■ How much would the house rent for?_____

■ And here's the million-dollar question: Do you have any other properties for sale? _____

Fill out a Property Analysis Worksheet like this on every call you make. I suggest doing all your real estate business this way, by making calls and completing the worksheet as you go.

> **These are two important numbers to know when you're considering buying a piece of property: (1) what the sellers bought the property for and (2) what the current mortgage amount is.**
>
> **Generally, people won't sell their property for less than what they bought it for or less than what the mortgage is. There are a few exceptions, especially when they're in financial trouble or when the bank is willing to make a short sale or discount the amount of money that's owed.**

Get Business to Come to You

Instead of your always sourcing and approaching sellers, it's better to have them come to you. In addition to developing referrals, use your imagination to come up with other ways to make business come to you. One of my students, James, came up with this method. He sets up a seminar at a local library, partnering with a good bankruptcy lawyer and mortgage broker. He advertises in the local paper, "If you're in foreclosure, about to lose your house, learn your rights." He conducts a 60- to 90-minute seminar and a handful of people show up. He usually gets one to two deals from every seminar.

Here's a sample ad:

If you're about to lose your house, learn your rights.
Come to this free seminar. No obligation.

Whenever you're talking to someone about a property, always ask, "Do you have any other property that you would like to sell?" I asked this of an older gentleman I had called in response to a For Rent ad. I had the impression that he had one rental property that he wanted to sell at a big discount. He was motivated because he wanted to retire. Then, I asked that one question, "Do you have any more?" He said, "Yes, I've got 88 other ones." He offered to sell them to me for 70 cents on the dollar. I flipped 45 of those properties over the next year, making an average of $8,500 on each! Imagine how much you can make by asking that question over the years.

Ten years ago, when I started in real estate, the newspapers were filled with notices of foreclosures. There were fewer buyers, and the market was not as hot as it is now. I used to look at five to eight properties and find a deal. Today, I consider between 50 and 150 properties to find a deal. Is all this trouble worth it? Absolutely. The only thing that matters is what one deal can be worth.

If you find a house in the $200,000 price range and you're able to make 10 percent for wholesaling it, that's $20,000 in your pocket. Of course, this ratio depends on your experience, the area you're in, and the type of real estate you're looking at. Track the number of phone calls you're making and your success rate. If you continue to follow these success plans, six months from today you'll discover that you're achieving a much higher success rate than you were your first week.

> *Experienced investors:* If you follow this 40-Day Action Plan in your business, your results could double or triple. Suppose that one deal is worth $5,000 to $100,000 or more. If you make that extra phone call or send just one more letter, even if it works only once, you could make a huge amount of money.

As you call people, remember to keep building your three lists: buyers, sellers, and people with money. To increase your business, always ask this magic question: Do you have anything else you want to sell? And always ask this question: Do you know anyone else who might have a property for sale, or who is buying property, or who has money? About one out of four times you ask that, you'll receive a referred lead. Most investors' new deals come from referrals, as many as 60 percent to 80 percent of them.

DAY 8   Action Plan

It's Up to You to Make It Happen!

Your goal is to spend two hours today making phone calls from the contacts you found in the newspaper. You can probably make between 20 to 30 phone calls in one hour. Make that your target rate.

✔ How many calls did you make?

_____

✔ How many people did you reach?

_____

✔ List any potential deals.

_____

_____

_____

_____

_____

_____

_____

✔ Who would you call to help you with an immediate deal if necessary?

_____

From now on, spend at least one hour a week making these phone calls. If you do this faithfully for 30 weeks, something will certainly happen. On the other hand, if you make phone calls for 30 minutes only one time, not much at all will happen.

_____

Making Phone Calls, Part 2

Today, you're making more phone calls. Block out 90 minutes to two hours and make 20 to 30 phone calls an hour. Some of these calls can be asking people to lunch to start building your team. Some of them can be to find those supersuccessful investors. All of them will pay off. You'll gain experience, grow in knowledge, or discover deals.

Time Management

Believe it or not, 60 percent to 80 percent of your business can be handled over the phone. You'll find, however, that people will ask you to meet with them. Ask them why. Adopt the attitude that you're very busy; you're a professional. You have a lot of phone calls to make, a lot of properties to buy, a lot of offers to present. So ask people why they want to meet—why can't you do business over the phone, through the fax, or via e-mail?

I've learned the most efficient use of my time is on the phone looking for deals. I can even have a contract signed or close on a property through a fax or by using a courier service. I avoid driving across town, and getting stuck in traffic. The first year or two I was in real estate, I didn't even think about all my driving, but then I began to analyze how I spent my time.

I calculated that being stuck in traffic ate up 80 percent of my time. I was driving to meet people that I didn't really have to meet. I was driving to the hardware store to pick up materials, driving to pick up pieces of paper. Now, I use the phone, fax, e-mail, and courier services, saving all that time!

How will you manage your time?

If you're taking someone to lunch to build your team, however, or you're working on a big real estate deal, then go ahead and take the time to meet in person. But try to do most of your business over the phone. Become sensitive of your time. If you drive across town to meet someone, that takes 30 to 40 minutes. Then you spend an hour or two in the meeting and another 40 minutes to drive back. Half of your day is gone. What could you have done with that half-day? How many phone calls could you have made in the time you spent driving?

The most frustrating part of running any business is reaching people. That's true in real estate, too. So, what should your expectations be of getting a hold of someone? Zero! If you contact someone, you ought to be thrilled! If you can leave a message on voicemail, you ought to be excited. And if someone actually calls you back, you ought to feel as if you've won the lottery. In reality, most people won't pick up the phone and call back. Keep making those calls, and set your expectations to zero. That way, you'll always be pleasantly surprised.

One of the keys to real estate investing is following up. Call people back. Make sure you reach them. Call them every business day, and leave a friendly, positive message until they call back. If you call only once, they may forget about your message or misplace their notes. But if you call several days in a row, they'll call you back, if only to make you stop calling!

Remember, real estate is competitive. If you don't call back, someone else will call in the interim. So pick up the phone, and make those calls.

Leaving Phone Messages

Often, you won't reach the people you're calling directly. Instead, you'll get their voicemail or answering service. These people don't know you, and they're not likely to call you back. Besides, people do what comes easiest, and answering a call is easier than making one. How do you entice them to make the effort to call you back? You leave a compelling message. And be sure to state your phone number slowly, repeating it for the listener to write down.

If you're calling about a For Sale ad, say, "I'm looking to buy two or three investment properties in the next 10 to 20 days." That tells them you're serious, and you build urgency.

If you're calling an investor about a For Rent ad say, "I'm looking to rent something very soon. I'm looking at a lot of other properties. Please call me back."

If you're calling real estate agents, say, "I'd like to buy two to three houses in the next 20 days, and I'm looking at a lot of property. Please call me back."

If you leave much more compelling messages, not just your name and phone number, you'll achieve a much better response rate. When you leave a phone number, direction, or address over the phone, speak slowly and repeat everything twice. As you record this type of information, actually *write it down as you say it*. Then you know you're speaking at a speed that will allow the other person to write down your message.

DAY 9   Action Plan

It's Up to You to Make It Happen!

✔ Spend an hour and a half to two hours making phone calls from the contacts you found in the newspaper. Remember, you can probably make between 20 to 30 phone calls in one hour. Set that number as your target rate.

How many calls did you make? _____

How many people did you reach? _____

List any potential deals here:

_____

_____

_____

_____

_____

_____

_____

✔ Landlords and investors are good people to talk to; you can learn from their successes and their mistakes. To help you learn, when you call on the investment property ads, ask the owners the following questions and write down their answers:

"How long have you been investing?" _____

"How do you like real estate investing?" _____

"I'm getting started, could I take you out to lunch?" _____

✔ At least once a week, take a successful real estate investor out to lunch.

Who will you take out to lunch this week? _____

Next week? _____

The following week? _____

The week after that? _____

Schedule these lunches as you make your calls on the ads.

Name: _____ Date:_____ Time:_____

Name: _____ Date:_____ Time:_____

✔ After you make your calls, write down these three things:

What did I learn today? Maybe you learned some market prices or found some players active in real estate in your area. Maybe you found some sellers, buyers, or resources. List them here.

_____

_____

_____

_____

_____

_____

_____

How could you make calls more efficiently? Is there anything you forgot to say? How could you leave a better message?

_____

_____

_____

_____

_____

_____

Did you enjoy making the calls? If not, how could you get someone else to do it?

_____

_____

Driving for Dollars, Part 1

Driving for dollars is another way to find potentially motivated sellers. Pick an area in transition in which you're interested, drive around, and look for homes with signs of motivation. How can you tell? Look for indications of neglect, such as tall grass, property showing massive need of repairs, condemned property wrapped with yellow tape—the worse the house, the better the deal. Look for real estate agents' For Sale signs, For Sale by Owner signs, and For Rent signs. Additionally, the smaller the sign, the better the deal, because no one else has seen it.

Not only can you find houses, you may also find commercial buildings or empty lots. Write all the information down. Then spend a little time doing research, because if you do enough, you'll find potential deals within the next 90 days. Again, one deal can be highly profitable.

Be persistent. You may have to call and call and call to find the owners. Start by calling the Registrar of Deeds, getting on the Internet, and going to the local tax records office to locate the owners. Ask a real estate professional to look up properties on the MLS computer. Then call or write to the owners once you find them.

Look for Indications of Neglect

Vacant Homes

If houses look deserted, or the grass is high and the bushes overgrown, could the owners possibly be motivated sellers? Absolutely. Put them on your list.

For Sale Signs

As you drive for dollars, look for For Sale and For Sale by Owner signs. Some of these signs might say Make Offer. Pay extra close attention to them. Because you are still driving through neighborhoods, learning about them, and finding potential deals, make a point of meeting the real estate agents who are active in these areas. You will learn a tremendous amount from talking with them and from carefully reading the signs.

For Rent Signs

If a house is for rent, you may locate a highly motivated landlord tired of managing it. Perhaps he bought the property 20 years ago for a fifth of what it's worth today. The best properties may be the empty ones. Call about these, too.

DAY 10   Action Plan

It's Up to You to Make It Happen!

✔ Spend your two hours today driving for dollars. Pick a neighborhood in transition, and drive around, getting to know it, gathering addresses. Find at least 20 addresses you can write down for neglected, vacant, or condemned homes. Or look for ones with signs saying For Sale, For Sale by Owner, or For Rent.

✔ How much time did you spend driving for dollars? _____

✔ How many addresses did you write down? _____

✔ List at least 20 addresses:

_____

_____

_____

_____

_____

_____

_____

_____

_____

_____

_____

_____

_____

_____

_____

_____

_____

_____

_____

_____

✔ Spend time doing research, then contact your leads.

How many letters or phone calls did you make? _____

How many responses did you get? _____

✔ Are any of the leads promising? How could you potentially make any money or find any deals from these people? _____

_____

_____

✔ Fill out a Property Analysis Worksheet for each lead. (See Day 8 for worksheet.)

Driving for Dollars, Part 2

On Day 11, you're driving for dollars again. Pick the same area but go to another part. Or pick another area and keep on driving. At this point, you can focus on houses with a particular profile. For example, look at vacant houses or properties with For Rent signs or For Sale signs. Spending time driving through an area and becoming familiar with it will pay off in the long run.

Remember, you've committed to spend an hour and a half to two hours each day on your real estate business. If you drive for dollars for two sessions, a total of three to four hours, you'll scope the neighborhoods and determine what's happening.

Broaden Your Horizons

If you're in a major metropolitan area, you may want to focus your research on an area near the edge of town or even in small towns nearby. You'll find a lot of op-

> **Set office hours. This is more than a recommendation; it's important advice for you and your family. The biggest problem with real estate investors—and entrepreneurs in general—is that they work too much. Work can be addictive. If you don't set office hours, your family life will suffer, your personal life will suffer, your spiritual life will suffer, and you'll make less money because you're working all the time. So set office hours. And stick to them. Do the work for the two hours you set aside, then quit and do what you're supposed to do—enjoy time with family and friends.**

portunity in the outskirts of cities, and the outskirts are usually less competitive than the city center.

At this point, let's broaden your horizons. You may be thinking only about houses and condominiums and duplexes. Some of my students have actually taken driving for dollars on farm land. They've put it under contract and wholesaled it. One of my students makes a lot of money by specializing in hunting camps that he wholesales to corporations. Another one of my students specializes in older driving ranges and golf courses in small towns. You may decide to look for smaller apartment buildings or houses in horrible shape. It's up to you to develop your specialty based on your research and interests.

Stay Safe

It's always better to drive for dollars with someone who's willing to help you. (Besides, it's more fun.) While you're driving, the other person can write down addresses for properties you might want to check out. Drive slowly, and make sure you get the correct address and phone numbers from the signs you see.

I wouldn't recommend knocking on doors. It could be dangerous; there may be vagrants or people on drugs using a vacant house. Instead, send letters and make phone calls. A lot of the owners of these properties can be hard to find. One way to find them is by asking neighbors. They often know what's going on. Another good tactic is asking postal workers in the neighborhood. They may have information about the house, where the owner is, and who currently lives there. They may even have a forwarding address.

DAY 11   Action Plan

It's Up to You to Make It Happen!

✔ When you spend your two hours today driving around, pick different neighbor-hoods in the beginning, and get to know them. Write down at least 20 ad-dresses of neglected, vacant, or condemned homes, or ones with signs saying For Sale, For Sale by Owner, or For Rent.

How much time did you spend driving for dollars? _____

How many addresses did you write down? _____

List the addresses here:

_____

_____

_____

_____

_____

_____

_____

_____

_____

_____

_____

_____

_____

_____

_____

_____

_____

_____

_____

_____

_____

_____

✔ Spend time doing research on the sellers, then contact them.

How many letters or phone calls did you complete? _____

How many responses did you get? _____

Are any of the leads promising? How could you potentially make any money or find any deals from these people? _____

_____

_____

✔ Fill out a Property Analysis Worksheet for each one. (See Day 8 for worksheet.)

Government Agencies, Part 1

On Day 12, you're still looking for motivated sellers, this time through the agencies of local and state governments.

It's All in the Public Record

Some real estate investors complain about the government: the IRS, courts, regulations. But I love the government. As a real estate investor, you should love the government, too, because it's hard at work making hundreds of thousands of motivated sellers and good deals for you.

All types of courts exist to help create motivated sellers (even when they didn't think they were motivated). My favorite agencies for finding motivated sellers are the codes court and the eviction court, as well as the other courts such as divorce court, probate court, and bankruptcy court.

Sources of Deals

Codes Court

Go to your local housing administration office to find out scheduled dates for the codes court, where landlords and investors go to defend their interests. The codes court enforces the codes and can issue fines. They can even condemn homes and have them bulldozed. You'll find that motivated sellers come to these courtrooms.

The proceedings are all in the public record. The docket for the day is usually posted outside of the courthouse. You can talk to owners while they are there, and meet with lawyers, landlords, and other investors who come. Chances are you'll find a good deal.

Go to the codes court, and just listen in for an hour or two. Meet some of the owners and attorneys as they're coming down after receiving fines and judgments for not making repairs. Ask if they're interested in getting rid of the property. Ask if the house is scheduled to be bulldozed next week. (You don't want to buy it on Tuesday and see it disappear four days later.) Use what you'll learn in Property

Dale, one of my successful students, is a full-time college student. Like you, he's very busy. He gets a list of the housing administration codes violations and sends a letter to the owners saying, "I understand you're having trouble with the city. I might be interested in buying your property from you and helping you get rid of this problem. Call me." He usually gets one or two deals from that list of 30 to 50 properties that are on the codes list.

After he puts them under contract, he runs an ad in the newspaper, saying, "Handyman Special." He directs potential buyers to drive by the property to check it out. Then, they make offers. He wholesales one house each month, making between $7,000 to $12,000 a month. That's all he's been doing for over a year. What's interesting is that his college professors probably spent $100,000 on their educations, then go to college and graduate school for 6 to 10 years and work on their master's degrees and doctorate theses. The average professor makes $40,000 to $75,000 a year. By way of contrast, Dale is a full-time student and makes more than $100,000 a year wholesaling one house a month from the codes list.

Analysis (see Days 18 and 19) to make sure you have a good deal. Understand the numbers, and be certain that you're able to do the repairs. Also make sure that you have enough time to either sell the property or make the repairs.

Eviction Court

Every major city has a busy eviction court. Who shows up there? Tenants, attorneys, landlords, and property managers. When owners have a conflict on their hands and have to go to court to resolve it, they could be in the market to sell for a good price.

When you go to eviction court, you may find some great deals but guaranteed you'll find better entertainment than any TV sitcom. Yes, the spectacle can be sad, but it's also entertaining to watch property managers and tenants present their cases, sometimes not very eloquently, in front of the judge. In many cases, the tenants haven't paid their rents and are being evicted. The property managers/landlords are motivated. They haven't received rent for several months and may have to deal with damage to their property. Many don't have proper policies and procedures to manage their property. Clearly, owning property is not working out as they wanted it to.

At eviction court, you can also network with people you want to know. I like to talk to landlords, to see if they're tired of managing their properties and would like to sell.

I suggest you take to lunch various property managers and the attorneys who represent them. I make a lot of deals from property managers I've met at eviction court. Since property managers are mainly interested in making money, you can offer to take over the property, manage it for them, and still pay them their management fee. Or if you buy the property, you can pay the property manager a commission. Sometimes, property managers have hundreds of scattered properties. They can help you buy them, but they won't want to sell them if they're going to lose money.

If you don't want to spend time at eviction court, you can get names, addresses, and phone numbers of people on the docket. As a public record, the list of evictions is posted on the outside of the eviction court. Send those people listed a letter that asks, "Do you have any properties you'd like to sell?" Then take steps to follow up.

Divorce Court

Because divorce records are public, you can actually look up case files and see what a couple owns. Many divorces have a home they must sell, and they're often willing to take a discount just to settle the assets and get out of the marriage quickly. I suggest getting to know some divorce attorneys, keep in touch with them, and show up at divorce court. Keep your eyes open for good possibilities in this venue.

Probate Court

You can look in the public records where deceased persons' assets are listed and then contact the attorneys and the families involved. You might say, "Would you like to unload these properties quickly? I can help you out." Do you think you can find deals that way? You bet.

Bankruptcy Court

Spend a few hours at the courthouse looking at bankruptcy files, and search for any real estate involved that might be sold. Get to know the people who work there. Tell them what you're doing. They will help you.

DAY 12 Action Plan

It's Up to You to Make It Happen!

✔ Your homework is to spend a couple of hours at the courthouse.

Call your local housing codes department. The phone number is _____.

List properties that have codes letters on them.

_____   _____
_____   _____
_____   _____

List people you met at the codes court and add them to your database:

_____   _____
_____   _____
_____   _____
_____   _____
_____   _____
_____   _____
_____   _____
_____   _____
_____   _____

✔ Find the eviction court, and sit in on the fun.

Try to meet at least five people at eviction court. List their names and contact information here.

_____   _____
_____   _____
_____   _____

✔ Find the divorce, probate, and bankruptcy courts. Look at the files to see if any real estate is involved. Get to know the people who work there. Tell them what you're doing. They'll become part of your team and help you find deals.

Who works at the courthouse in divorce court? _____

Who works in the probate court? _____

Who works in the bankruptcy court? _____

Government Agencies, Part 2

The government potentially provides a lot of motivated sellers for you. A lot of people use traditional ways to find good deals in real estate. Let me be clear about this: All the methods work. You can pick one or two methods, such as foreclosures, short sales, tax sales, driving for dollars, and make any of them work with experience. But, the competition these days is stepping up.

Pick another court or government agency to visit. In addition to the ones covered on Day 12, your options include the local tax office for IRS liens, local property tax sales, and environmental court.

Tax Sales and IRS Liens

If people don't pay their property taxes, the government taxing entity will demand payment and force a tax foreclosure. You can buy the property at a tax sale, or, in certain states, you can buy a tax certificate for the amount of the back taxes. By

> Wait a minute! Now that the word is out in this book, everyone will start to go to the courthouse to look for deals, and it won't be such a good source anymore! Are you worried about that? Consider this: Even though a lot of people get excited about real estate and understand how to do it, even *say* they'll do it, the truth is, most people *won't* do it. I hope that you're different and special, and that you'll go out and do some of these things you're reading about. Sure, there's competition, but there's plenty of room for more.
>
> Here's more food for thought: When I call about an ad, I always ask if any other real estate investors have called. Most of the time they say, "Nope. You're the only one." So be assured, there's plenty of room out there for you. Don't be among those people who learn something and get excited, but never actually do anything. That's why this book gives you step-by-step action plans. Now you can go out and make it happen.

using a certificate, you get interest on your money or on the property. Some tax certificates pay anywhere from 10 percent to 30 percent interest.

People buy at tax sales for two reasons:

(1) They hope to get the property for the amount of back taxes due. For example, if a $200,000 house has $8,000 of property taxes not paid and goes to a tax sale, investors want to buy it for $8,000, the amount of the back taxes. Of course, several investors bidding can actively raise the price, but you can still find good deals at tax sales.

(2) Many cities, counties, and states by law demand that the taxes owed and the amount bid collect a good interest rate. In certain areas, every taxing authority has rules and laws for how sales are run. Some require as much as 20 percent to 30 percent interest paid. For example, say the owner of a house worth $200,000 owes $8,000 in back taxes. You bid $8,000 with the intent to acquire the house for the amount of taxes only. However, your city has a one-year right of redemption rule, which means the homeowner has one year to pay back all the taxes and interest due, and can legally redeem the property.

In this example, say your area's interest rate for tax liens is 20 percent and the homeowner pays you $8,000 plus 20 percent to get the house back. If the homeowner doesn't pay you off within one year, you get to keep the $200,000 home. However, you can't sell that house until the year is up.

Alternatively, you could buy properties for the amount of the tax lien. You can also acquire them by bidding on them at a foreclosure sale auction.

Between the time you hear of a pending tax sale or foreclosure and before it happens, you should talk to the property owners affected. Are they motivated to sell? Yes. Are they hard to talk to sometimes? Yes, because people have a psychological defense mechanism called *denial*. Sometimes people say, "No, I don't want to talk to you. I'm going to win the lottery. Someone will show up at my door and give me a million dollars. I know it's going to happen, so leave me alone."

Sure, they may be difficult to talk with, but most often the things that are hardest to obtain are the sweetest. So work these foreclosures and preforeclosure tax sales.

Environmental Court

People who leave too much junk on their properties wind up in the environmental court. The judge fines people for not removing trash and not cleaning their yards. Owners of these properties can be highly motivated to sell. Go meet them, get their names, and contact them afterward, because they could turn into good deals.

Advanced Sources of Deals

If you're having trouble finding deals through the traditional methods of foreclosure and bankruptcy, and you are already an experienced real estate investor, try the next two sources.

Mold-Damaged Properties

One of the hottest areas of litigation right now is mold. In many areas of the country, houses are growing mold; people are getting sick and can't live in them. Numerous lawsuits and insurance claims involving mold are in the courts. An experienced real estate investor can focus on mold houses. You can hire professional firms that will guarantee mold removal. Sometimes, it's not as expensive to get the mold out as you might think.

One of my students, Andrea, has found a contractor who can remove mold inexpensively. She finds owners of houses that have insurance claims for mold problems. These owners are highly motivated to sell. She makes an offer based on what the property is worth minus her mold expert's bid. She's getting incredible deals buying these houses, fixing them, and getting letters of guarantee from contractors that the mold has been removed and the houses have become healthy.

Properties Damaged by Fire or Water

Houses with fire or water damage claims make up another area to specialize in. The gentleman who got me started in real estate specialized in houses that had suffered fire or water damage. Often, the owners had collected on a large insurance claim, so they'd received money for a good part of the house and were ready to move. They were willing to sell the house at a deep discount because the house had basically been paid for through the insurance settlement.

DAY 13   Action Plan

It's Up to You to Make It Happen!

✔ Your homework is to spend a few hours at the courthouse.

Where do the tax sale lien books exist? Note places here:

_____

_____

✔ Talk to the registrar of deeds, title searchers, lawyers, and people representing banks and mortgage companies. Exchange business cards. Build your database. Ask them to keep an eye out for deals for you. At some point, put them on your team. List the names and contact numbers of people you met here:

_____

_____

_____

_____

_____

✔ Visit the environmental court. List the names and contact numbers of any prospective sellers you found here.

_____

_____

_____

_____

_____

Networking, Part 1

There are only so many houses you can look at and only so many phone calls you can make. So consider one of the best ways to find deals: networking.

What types of people can help you find deals? You've already read about some of them: real estate agents, accountants, financial planners, appraisers, bankers and mortgage brokers, attorneys, people who work foreclosures, bankruptcy trustees, home inspectors, contractors, repair people, utility workers, postal workers, police officers, and other investors. Ask all of these people to look out for deals that they'd be willing to pass on to you. Read on to learn why you'll want these people on your team.

Your Real Estate Team

Real Estate Agents

Real estate agents have access to the Multiple Listing Service (MLS) and to buyers and sellers, so get to know the active agents in your targeted areas. When good deals come their way, they will call someone, and that someone should be you. Make sure they get paid when they find deals, so that you keep your relationships golden. By the way, if I use agents and brokers but do not close on a property with them, I give them a check for their time until they find me something. It keeps the relationship solid.

CPAs, Accountants, Bookkeepers

When people want to do financial planning, settle their estate, sell some property, raise money, or get out of financial trouble, they turn to their trusted accountant or financial planner. These professionals often help clients dispose of their property, so get to know them and build your network.

Bankers and Mortgage Brokers

Bankers and brokers make loans to real estate people and often know where good deals are. Because they have access to funds, they may be able to finance the good deals you find. They also know lots of other investors and can help you expand your network.

When people get into financial trouble—heading for bankruptcy or foreclosure—they follow a predictable pattern of behavior. They run to their accountants, mortgage brokers, and financial planners. In desperation, they might call a real estate agent and say, "Can you sell my house in three weeks?" As a last resort, they call a bankruptcy attorney.

Because of this pattern, you want to build a network of mortgage bankers, real estate agents, accountants, and attorneys so that when desperate people call, they will send them to you. You can pay them cash for their house, quick-turn it, make money yourself, and possibly stop them from going bankrupt.

Attorneys

Attorneys manage a lot of things that can help your business, such as estate sales, divorce, bankruptcy. Find several active attorneys in your area and network with them.

Contractors

All contractors, big or small, look at properties that need work. They know owners, and some of those owners will be motivated to sell. So contact every contractor and repairperson you know and say, "If you bring me a deal that I close on, I will pay you a finder's fee."

Utility Workers

Utility workers—from the gas company, electric company, water company, and so on—are walking and driving in neighborhoods every day. They know a lot about houses, neighborhoods, and the people they deal with. They might be able to say, "Hey, I know about a house that needs a lot of work. We recently had to shut the gas (or the water) off. And here's the owner and address."

Post Office Workers

Often postal workers know more about you and your neighbors than you think. They know who is getting divorced, who is moving, who has to sell a house. In fact, some successful real estate investors are post office workers. Ask them to help you identify good deals.

Police Officers

Police officers have a tough job in the neighborhoods. They learn about houses or properties that must be sold, especially ones they just locked up because somebody did something naughty inside. Police officers may be able to point you to motivated sellers.

Nursing Home Workers

Our population is getting older, and more people are moving into retirement homes, assisted living units, and nursing homes. Often, people are forced to sell their property and their assets to qualify for financial assistance before going into a home.

Real Estate Associations

Most major cities have a real estate association or a landlord association. Who attends their meetings? Investors, landlords, and people who find good deals. Associations are great sources of education, too. At www.sheminrealestate.com we provide a list of real estate associations. Network at their meetings, and you will find everything you need to become a successful real estate investor.

Other Investors

You find these people through real estate associations and through I Buy Houses ads. If an ad says, "We loan money on real estate" or "We buy houses," follow through because these investors will become your favorite people. Sometimes, they may find more deals than they know what to do with; they'll pass some on to you,

> One of my students hangs out at nursing homes to find good deals. He makes friends with the administrators, who call him and say, "Mrs. Smith has to sell her home, and the family doesn't want to deal with it. Can you help them out?" He gets a lot of good deals that way. He's not taking advantage of the situation; he's truly helping them. And he discloses in writing exactly what he is doing.

> **Of all the ways to find good deals that I've listed here, the best ones in my experience have proven to be these three:**
>
> 1. **Finance companies**
> 2. **Disgruntled landlords**
> 3. **Other investors**

and you can later pass some on to them. As a matter of fact, I'd say that 80 percent to 90 percent of all the wholesale deals I complete are partnered with other investors. Sometimes, it is possible to do double and triple flips if there's enough margin in the deals.

Be sure to network and meet people who are in the investment business. Affiliate yourself with the good ones, and your business will grow.

Tired Landlords

If landlords are not managing their property properly, they're going to have headaches and stress, and they won't be making a profit. They may be burned out. They may be motivated to sell. They'll likely give you big discounts for taking the problem off their hands.

Pay a Little, Make a Lot

Find as many of these people as you can, and let them know you're working on building your real estate business. If you can do so legally and ethically, pay them when you close on a deal they send your way.

I have flyers and cards that say, "If you help me find a house and I close, I'll pay you at least $500 cash at closing." If I wholesale a property and make $8,000, I might pay them $750 or $1,000. I give out the cards and flyers to all the people listed above.

You can take a few to lunch and educate them on what you're looking for: houses that need repairs, people who are sick of their property, and so on.

It's the strangest thing. A lot of people in real estate have not figured this out. They like to be greedy and not pay people who help them. So they make a little extra money on one deal, but don't do a lot of deals. I've discovered one of the most interesting secrets in business: If you pay people and do what you say you're going to do, they want to keep doing business with you.

One repairperson has brought me more than 30 deals. One real estate agent has brought me over 40 deals. A fellow investor has brought me over 12 deals. I've sold over 80 properties to another investor. I make sure that he always makes money on every deal. In other words, I don't squeeze out every last dollar. Instead of making $8,000, I only make $4,000. But then he's making money and still wants to do business with me. I recommend that you adopt this successful business philosophy.

Network with everyone you can. Let people know you're looking for deals. You'll be amazed. At some point, everyone knows people who have got to sell their property fairly quickly and may be motivated.

DAY 14 Action Plan

It's Up to You to Make It Happen!

Who should be in your business network?

✔ Contact five to seven people you want to network with. What kind of response did you get? Record it.

Contact _____ Response _____

Contact _____ Response _____

Contact _____ Response _____

Contact _____   Response _____

Contact _____   Response _____

Contact _____   Response _____

Contact _____   Response _____

Networking, Part 2

Spend another day building your network. Go down the list from Day 14 and find another five to seven people you'd like to network with. Call them. Meet with them. Take them to lunch to educate them about the kind of deals and sellers you're looking for: properties with signs of motivation, such as For Sale by Owner signs, houses that need work—not just every house that has a sign in the yard. You can give them a Property Analysis Worksheet to fill out, if you'd like. Put in writing that if they bring you a deal you close on, you'll pay them whatever you think makes sense in your business.

Always continue to expand your network. Keep handing out those cards and flyers, and pay people quickly. Know that the first time you give them a handful of cash, they'll get busier and find you even more deals.

Build a Referral Circle

If you're talking to someone who is in foreclosure and you can't help him because he owes $200,000 and his house is worth $190,000, and the bank will not discount the mortgage, what do you do? Instead of hanging up on him, you can refer (not necessarily recommend) desperate homeowners in financial trouble back to professionals in your network. These professionals help you find deals, and you help them build their businesses. And you're even helping the homeowner. Over time, this will build your business reputation. You'll start getting referrals, and your business will grow, grow, grow!

DAY 15   Action Plan

It's Up to You to Make It Happen!

Who should be in your business network?

✔ Contact five to seven people you want to network with. What kind of response did you get? Record it.

Contact	_____	Response	_____
Contact	_____	Response	_____
Contact	_____	Response	_____
Contact	_____	Response	_____
Contact	_____	Response	_____
Contact	_____	Response	_____
Contact	_____	Response	_____

Negotiating, Part 1

Would you like to know how to double your income? If by negotiating, I can show you how to save $1.00, what would you have to make working at a regular job to save the same amount? About $1.50 to $2.00 depending on the city and state where you live, and the tax bracket you're in. You can double your income by learning how to save money and by negotiating, too. I assure you, the most money you'll ever make will come from negotiating.

Basics of Negotiating Skills

1. Build rapport with other people.
2. Disarm them by being personable.
3. Find out what their real needs are. What are their pains?

4. Ask open-ended questions.

5. Find out if they'll accept less than the asking price.

Build Rapport

When you start talking with someone about a property, be nice. People like to do business with people they like. To build rapport, use humor, be yourself, ask questions about them: where they live, what type of work they do, what's their family situation, what they like to do for fun. Let them talk; just ask questions.

Disarm Them

When you get down to business, disarm them, which means make them feel comfortable. You do that by "pacing" or paying attention to people's reality, so whatever you suppose is on their minds, mention it up front. For example, if their house is in foreclosure, say, "I know a lot of people are calling you and bothering you. You're probably under a lot of stress." That statement helps to disarm the person you're calling who stops and thinks, "Wait a minute. This person understands me."

When talking with a homeowner, say, "Look, I know you have to sell your house quickly, and I know you're unsure about what you want to do. You probably don't want to talk about it, or tell me this information, but I'm trying to help."

Take just a minute to think about what people might be thinking, what their real pain or problem is, and address it up-front. Ask why they must sell this home. What would they do with the money? Get specific details.

> Try this disarming approach the next time you're at a restaurant and get a bad meal. You'll find that yelling at the waiter won't do any good because he's not the restaurant's main decision maker, and yelling doesn't usually get anyone anywhere. Instead, *pace the waiter's reality* and say, "I know you have a lot of tables to wait on." Learn whatever his reality is at the time. That will put him at ease and make it easier to talk about your concern.

Find Their Pain

Say I'm calling on a potential lease-option deal. I'm trying to lease option the property from the landlord, so I'll ask her, "What don't you like about the rental property?" She might say, "I don't like collecting the rent, I'm tired of the repairs, and I never get any free time, I don't have the weekends off." I probe further: "If you didn't have the property and had some money, what would you do?" She might say, "I'd love to travel, go fishing, spend more time with my family."

Find out what people really want. Then, when you go back to negotiate, always point out how they'll get what they want. For example, to the landlord mentioned earlier, I'd say, "If we could work this out, you'd have more free time to take trips, fish, and spend time with your family." Find out what they really want and what they really need. People usually say, "I just need the money." Most investors stop there. But not you. You're going to become an expert negotiator and gather information. Ask them what they're going to do with the money; then work their answers back into the negotiation.

Ask Open-Ended Questions

When it comes time to ask how much money they really want for the property, abide by this rule: The first person who mentions a number loses. So if you offer $200,000 on a house that's worth $300,000, the least you'll get that house for is $200,000, because you can't go down. What if they would have taken $180,000? You've not given them that opportunity.

My father always says I should be in much better shape because I'm always jumping to conclusions. When you're negotiating, don't jump to any conclusions or assume anything. Remove yourself from the process.

> If someone asks me, "What would you like to buy the house for?" I never mention a number. Instead, I tell them, "Look, I don't like to negotiate. I'm not very good at it." I speak slowly and pause, then say, "Without negotiating, what's the least you'd take for this property and be okay?" Then I'm silent. That silence is as short as one second; other times, it's as long as 20 seconds. The most powerful negotiating technique is silence.

If you determined the house was worth $300,000 and they want $250,000, most people would say, "That's a great deal! I'll take it!" But when you're negotiating, show no emotion. Never say anything about the house, good or bad, because it's their house.

Suppose you said, "This is a great house. I've got to have it. If I could just get this house, my investment career would really take off." You'd be giving them too much information. *Your job is to gather information, not give it out.*

Or if you say, "This house is a piece of junk. It's an awful neighborhood; I don't know why anyone would ever live there. I wouldn't pay any more than $100,000 for it, even though you say it's worth $300,000." That's very rude. Keep in mind you're talking about their home.

Rather than saying anything emotional, be disinterested. Tell them you're looking at several houses and will be making a lot of offers this week, so you really need to move on.

Will They Take Less?

Here's where the negotiation starts to look like what most people think of as negotiation—the back and forth banter. But remember, you started negotiating from your very first contact as you started building rapport.

To continue our example, usually people come back with a number. They say they'll take $250,000 for it. Maybe that's a decent deal for you. But don't get excited. Instead, say, "Seriously, what's the least you'd take and be okay?" Ask the question again. Give them another chance. About 20 percent to 30 percent of the time, they'll reduce their number. Then ask a third time, "Okay, really, without negotiating, what would be the absolute least you'd take and be okay?"

If they get upset, use another tool of negotiating called *reframing the negotiation.* Use humor to diffuse the situation. Smile and make light of it, saying, "I read this book about negotiating, and the author said to ask the question three times. Can you believe that? I thought he was kind of crazy, too." Laugh and smile, take a breather, then say, "So what would be the least you'd take for this house," and go right back into the negotiation.

When they get to the point where they say that's their rock-bottom price, that's when you first mention a number. It's called a test number. Go low, and use an odd number to throw them off. For example, say, "I was thinking more along the lines of $176,817." They might say, "No way, I want $235,000"; or "Look, there's no way I can do that, but I tell you what, I'll come down to $230,000." Or they could become upset, feeling insulted at such a low offer.

If they become upset, reframe the negotiation by saying, "The guy in the book said to throw out a low number. It's crazy. I'm sorry about that. Is there anything you can do?"

At this point, you're only negotiating on price. Later, you'll also negotiate on terms, closing costs and time, and anything else that might be involved with selling the property. If they do come down in price, consider that a reset button. They've reset the entire negotiation, and you start it all over again.

In your discussion, bring up their core values, what they want to do with the money—whatever their pain or problem is, then go back to negotiating. "What's the least you'll take?" Of course, you've got to read them well. If they tell you to not ask that question again, don't ask it. Often, prices are settled by splitting the difference, so be open to that possibility.

Once you've settled on a fee, start negotiating the terms, saying, "Okay, I'll pay you $219,000 for the house, but I'd like to just take over the mortgage payments. How's that?" After negotiating on owner's terms, then negotiate on the closing costs and request they pay all of them. Always ask for that. You may not get them to agree, but if you never ask, you'll never get.

DAY 16   Action Plan

It's Up to You to Make It Happen!

Practice your negotiating skills. Today, on Day 16, go out and buy something. It could be lunch, dinner, or something at a major store. Follow these instructions:

- First, find the decision maker. It's usually the manager.

- Second, build rapport. Compliment the manager on the restaurant or store.

- Third, appeal to the person by saying, "I know this is kind of strange to ask, but do you ever do anything special for good customers? Give them a discount or have any sales going on soon?" See if you can negotiate even better deals. Your rule from now on is ABN=Always Be Negotiating. If you go to a store and save anywhere from $30 to $5,000, it's money in your pocket. You'll be amazed at how many times people comply and give you more than you'd imagine.

- Fourth, ask this open-ended question: What do you do for good customers? Be silent, and let them answer the question.

- Fifth, when they offer something, ask for a bit more. "That's very nice. Thanks for the free dessert. Could we get two?" Now, don't be greedy, but why not ask? As it says in the Bible, "Ask and ye shall receive." Similarly, my rules of negotiating say, "Ask and you might receive." If you never ask, you'll never get.

Homework: Negotiate for one thing that you're going to buy.

✔ What did you want?

_____

_____

✔ What did you get?

_____

_____

✔ What did you learn?

_____

_____

_____

✔ How did you feel? (Were you nervous? Was the experience fun or exciting?)

_____

_____

Negotiating, Part 2

Follow and learn from some of the best negotiators in the world: children. If you don't have children of your own, find friends who have children between the age of 5 to 12, and ask them about negotiating. The greatest negotiating gift that children have is persistency. They never quit. Just ask their parents.

Child's Play

Ask children about negotiating: How do they get the toys they want, how do they get their ice cream, how do they get to stay up late?

You'll find they use almost all the negotiating techniques that were covered on Day 16. When children want something, first they build rapport by putting on their sweet face. They smile and tell their parents something funny, saying, "By the way, I was wondering if I could get ice cream today." If the mother says no, what does the child say? He uses the next negotiating tool. He asks why. If she says, "Because

My 11-year-old son asked what I was doing on a particular weekend. I told him I was going to teach negotiating at a real estate seminar. He said, "Negotiating? With adults? That's easy. Every kid knows how to do that." I asked him if he had any tips to share. He said, "Always put on your cute face. Always ask for more than you want. So if you want one Transformer, ask for three. If they say no, ask them why five to seven times. Then, if they won't let you have three, ask for two. If they won't let you have two, ask for one. And if they won't let you have anything now, ask for later."

Then he used one of the trickiest negotiating techniques in the world, saying, "If your mom won't give it to you, go to your dad." So if you're negotiating with one person who won't give you what you want, then go to somebody else, like the other spouse or another owner of the property. If you can, come back and never stop negotiating. "Then," he said, "when you do finally get an answer, if they let you have one toy, go back to the original request and ask, 'then why can't I have three?'" See this persistency? Incredible. It wears people down.

I told you that you can't have it," then the child again comes back with another "Why?" They usually ask why from three to eight times. They're negotiating. Then if the mom gets upset and threatens to punish him, the child reframes the request—another negotiating tool. He puts on his cute face, or starts crying, or laughing—whatever he's learned will get his mom out of that emotional state. Then he goes right back into negotiating, "Well, could I have ice cream tomorrow?" This persistence definitely pays off—for kids, at least.

So on Day 17, consult with a child and his parent about his technique. Afterward, go out into your community and negotiate for two or three things that you're going to buy or use. Then apply this in your real estate business in every transaction. Negotiate with your contractors, mortgage brokers, real estate agents, and sellers.

Good Cop/Bad Cop

Another negotiation technique is to use the Good Cop/Bad Cop negotiating tool. This is how it works: When negotiating with sellers who wants something that you don't want to give, say, "I've got to check with my partner; he's tough"; or say,

For success, focus on three things:

1. **Find a motivated seller.**
2. **Get a signed contract (without that, you have nothing).**
3. **Go to closing.**

   Those are your three focuses. If something you're doing doesn't further one of these three steps, it is probably a waste of your time.

"Gee, I wish I could get you full price for your house, but my partner won't allow it." Remove yourself from the process, so they're not upset with you. It's never you pushing. It's your partner.

Don't Give Up

People may say they won't negotiate, but they will. Give them your phone number. It could be a week or even a month later before they call, but some people are willing to negotiate if something changes.

Don't give up if people hang up on you, either. Wait 30 minutes to an hour, let them cool down, and call them back. Pace their reality, saying, "I know you don't like negotiating. I don't like it either. I know you're a little uncomfortable. You probably got upset. I'm very sorry about that. So, what can we do here?" And go right back into negotiating. Remember, silence and patience can be very effective.

Have a folder on every property with a deal sheet (name, address, info you found). Review these folders every 30 to 60 days, call the sellers up, or shoot them an offer—make some type of contact. Again, people who aren't motivated today might become motivated down the road.

If you don't like to negotiate, find someone who does. If you know someone who is a great negotiator, someone who likes to go bargain hunting at garage sales, someone who's good at making deals, partner with her.

Be aware of the style of the person you're negotiating with. If he or she is impatient, you've got to be more careful. You don't want to be offensive or develop any conflict. The moment people seem to feel nervous or uncomfortable, you have to do something to put them at ease. I recommend leaving the negotiation and talking about something else (what they do for a living, what they do for fun), then going back to negotiating.

In real estate, I've been in negotiations where someone wouldn't negotiate at all. The person said, "I want $1 million. That's it." At that point, you must make a business decision to go along or give up. Another option is to write up a low offer, shoot it over, and see what happens.

I've also been in negotiations on a larger piece of real estate that took three weeks of this kind of communication. It wasn't until the second week that we learned the real reason the sellers were selling—extremely important information. Keep in mind that on most of the property you'll buy, you *won't* find out why the sellers were really selling or what they would really take. Always ask yourself, "How much money did I leave on the table?"

You see, when you're negotiating, you're gathering information. If you've made an offer on a property and the offer is accepted, the only thing you learned is that you offered too much.

Realize that nothing in your life works all the time. I promise, however, that if you never use these skills, they'll never work. If you use them all of the time, they'll work some of the time. But the rewards can be huge. Because real estate deals are big-ticket items, by using negotiation principles, you can save from $1,000 to $100,000. Negotiating is worth attempting, even if it only works 20 percent to 30 percent of the time over your real estate investing career.

DAY 17 Action Plan

It's Up to You to Make It Happen!

Today, negotiate for two or three things that you're going to buy.

✔ What did they offer you?

_____

_____

✔ What did you get?

_____

_____

✔ How did you do it?

_____

_____

✔ How did you feel?

_____

_____

✔ Did you miss any steps? Did you build rapport and ask "what's the least you'd take" or "can you do any better" three times? What could you do differently next time?

_____

_____

_____

_____

_____

_____

_____

_____

_____

_____

_____

_____

Property Analysis, Part 1

The first 17 days of these action plans were designed to get you to look for motivated sellers and learn how to talk to them. Now you have to determine whether the deal you've found is good.

What Is a Good Deal?

Ten years ago, I would have said any property that you can get at 30 percent to 50 percent below what it's worth is a good deal. But markets are always changing. They've become more competitive. Today, if you can find a property that's 20 percent to 30 percent below market, you've found a good deal. Similarly, if a property will sell for $100,000 and you can buy it for $78,000 and no repairs are needed, that would be a decent deal.

Something is always out of kilter in the real estate market. Many years ago, there were a lot of properties for sale (a lot of motivated sellers), but there wasn't a lot of money out there (buyers). The good news was that *there were a lot of deals*.

The bad news was that *they were very hard to sell or it was hard to find people with enough money to buy them*. Right now, money and buyers are in abundance, but deals aren't. The good news is that when you find a deal, it's very easy to sell it. The bad news is, the deals are hard to find.

Don't let the market generalities stop you from investing, but certainly become aware of them.

Will You Know It When You See It?

You will, because you'll use this system to analyze properties. This same analysis applies to any type of property, whether it's a house, condominium, trailer, shopping center, or apartment building. There are basically three numbers you need to know:

1. What is the property worth today?
2. What will the needed repairs cost?
3. What can you get the property for?

What Is the Property Worth Today?

That is, what will someone pay for it? How do you determine that? If you hire an appraiser, you'll get three to five comparable sales of similar properties (close in size, location, type) that have sold recently. You can also go on the Internet to glean information. For links to free appraisal sites, go to www.sheminrealestate.com.

Suppose you're looking at a three-bedroom, two-bath house. Three houses like it on that same street just sold for $450,000. That means this house is probably worth $450,000, too, so be sure you're comparing apples to apples. No, you can't compare a house in the best neighborhood to a house eight miles away in a worse neighborhood. Similarly, you can't compare old to new or big to little. Look at all the variables when making comparisons.

Honestly, I don't put a lot of stock in comparable sales. I've seen properties comp at $800,000, but never saw anyone pay more than $700,000 for them. So in addition to running comps, verify the prices with a market professional—someone who buys and sells a lot of property in that area. That's why these action plans have you continually building your network with real estate agents and other investors.

If you're buying in a particular area and you know any agents who sell a lot of houses in that neighborhood, call and get their opinions about the comps. They'll be able to give you the scoop and may say perhaps that the market is slow right now and therefore the house won't sell for the comp price. Or they may have buyers who will pay more than the asking price because it's a hot market.

I recommend that you get everything in writing. Get your three to five comparable sales, and then also verify the price with a market professional until you feel comfortable that you can sell that property for that particular amount.

What Will the Needed Repairs Cost?

At this point, you're only analyzing properties that look good. They've already passed your initial test. You've talked to the sellers. They're motivated. The deal sounds good. There aren't many repairs. So you've put it under contract. You'll have a contingency clause in your contract, so you're not obligated to buy it.

Now is the time to do the rest of your due diligence, to make sure the repairs will cost what you'd estimated. How do you find out? Have a referred contractor go to the property and give you a realistic bid.

A couple of things can happen. The contractor can find that instead of the $10,000 in repairs you estimated, no repairs are needed. Or he could find more repairs totaling $15,000. Or he could determine that the property is falling apart and it will take $100,000 to fix it. The sellers either didn't know the extent of the repairs needed, or they lied to you. Is that a problem? No. Just go back and renegotiate. Keep emotion out of your real estate deals; negotiating is just numbers. Simply ask the sellers to renegotiate. If they won't, it's still not a problem because you have that contingency clause in your contract, which means you can walk away from the deal.

What Can You Get the Property For?

Determining this is where your negotiating skills really come into play. Study the negotiation techniques outlined in Days 16 and 17, and apply what you've learned at this point in your property analysis.

You want this important number to be as low as possible. That's why it's so critical to find a motivated seller.

What about Cash Flow and Return on Investment?

Worth, repairs, and cost—those are the only three numbers you need to get started in real estate. Advanced investors might also look at cash flow and return on investment (ROI). But even then, you've got to find a good deal, first and foremost. What if the rents don't go up or the market goes down, and you bought the property for full price? You probably won't be able to sell it.

Don't buy property that generates cash flow (the rent is greater than the expenses) just to have that cash flow. This is a book about real estate *investing*, not about real estate *speculation*. Those are two different things.

I don't like risk, so I buy property 20 percent to 30 percent below market price. This strategy spread protects you even if the real estate market falters, because it's unusual for the market to go down 30 percent or more.

DAY 18 Action Plan

It's Up to You to Make It Happen!

✔ Find two to three referred contractors (referred from investors, landlords, and others you've been networking with).

_____   _____

_____   _____

✔ Find a way to get comparable sales: You can do your research on the Internet or use your team—real estate agents and mortgage brokers. What method will you use?

_____

✔ Build your list of market professionals working in specific areas. These are people you can call to verify what the value of a particular property is.

Area		Contact	
Area	_____	Contact	_____
Area	_____	Contact	_____
Area	_____	Contact	_____
Area	_____	Contact	_____
Area	_____	Contact	_____
Area	_____	Contact	_____
Area	_____	Contact	_____
Area	_____	Contact	_____
Area	_____	Contact	_____

Advanced Property Analysis

G et in the habit of analyzing every property you call on. Use this Advanced Property Analysis Worksheet on the following page.

One way to determine what a house is worth is to run an ad and see if it attracts any interested buyers. I've also used ghost ads to determine the right rents and sales prices on properties for which I haven't found accurate comps. If no one calls on the ad in two weeks, you've learned something important: You've priced it too high. If your phone rings off the hook, then you have some idea of what buyers want. Only run ghost ads after you have the property under contract complete with a contingency clause to protect you.

Advanced Property Analysis Worksheet

Name of seller _____

Address of property _____

Type of property:

    Single family/multifamily _____   Number of units _____

    Square footage _____ Bedrooms_____   Bath _____

    Special features or comments:

_____

_____

Why the sellers are selling:

_____

_____

Their motivation on a scale from 0–10 _____

How long they have to close _____

The debt on the property _____

The three most important numbers:

1. What will the property sell for today? _____

    Comp _____   Market professional who verified _____

    Comp _____   Market professional who verified _____

    Comp _____   Market professional who verified _____

    Comp _____   Market professional who verified _____

    Comp _____   Market professional who verified _____

2. Cost of repairs detailed by contractor _____

3. Price seller will sell property for _____

    In addition, what special terms or conditions does the seller require? (For example, if you can get owner financing, what will the down payment and monthly payments be, what will the property rent for, how long do you think it will take to sell, how long will it take to rent?)

_____

_____

Use this sheet for a quick analysis to see whether you've found a good deal.

Do You Have Paralysis of Analysis?

If you're taking too long to analyze property, focus like a laser beam on the only three numbers you really need: What is the property worth today? What will the needed repairs cost? What can you get the property for?

The minute you find a deal, get on the Internet. Then call your real estate friends to get those three to five comparable sales and have them faxed or e-mailed over. All this should take between a few hours to two days. This first number tells you what the property is worth today.

To determine the repair number, ask the sellers what they think the repairs will cost; then send a referred contractor over to make an independent estimate. That will take one to three days.

Once you get the deal under contract, how can you determine what the real sales price is? The minute someone signs a contract with you, immediately send potential buyers over. That's the only way to really find out what a particular property is worth. I contact all my real estate friends, all my buyers, and other investors from my list. You'll be creating your own buyers list too as you call on ads in the newspaper and meet people at your real estate association. Send them over, and ask what they'd pay for this property.

For example, you may think it's worth $500,000 and have comps in hand to support that amount. Say that you have it under contract for $400,000 and it doesn't need any repairs. If the next day, your educated contacts go by and determine that no one is likely to pay more than $350,000 for it, then you've got a problem.

Appraising property and valuing properties is an art, not a science. Unless you have 100 houses that are exactly the same that are always selling, you can't determine market pricing precisely.

That's actually great news. It's only because real estate is an imperfect market that we're able to make a profit! Every piece of property has a 5 percent to 10 percent—sometimes even 15 percent—fudge factor built into the price. A house might be appraised at $300,000, but someone might pay $330,000 for it. A property might be appraised for $600,000, but no one will pay more than $575,000 for it. There's always a bit of leeway; you'll never get an exact comparable market price. That's why real estate investing is regarded as an art.

The only way you can really tell you what a property is worth is to check the market. Don't wait or wonder. Don't let paralysis of analysis set in. Instead, pick up the phone and dial 7 to 10 numbers; get someone to help you. *Any time you get paralyzed, take action.*

DAY 19   Action Plan

It's Up to You to Make It Happen!

Find two properties to practice your analysis skills on. Discover what they are worth, what the repairs are, and what you can get them for. Fill out your worksheet. Become comfortable finding comparable sales. Then, when the real deal comes up, you'll be ready to take action.

1. Which two properties did you analyze?

    Property #1: _____

    Property #2: _____

2. What were the results?

    Property #1: Worth _____   Property 2: Worth _____

    Repairs _____   Repairs _____

    Cost _____   Cost _____

3. Do you think they might turn out to be good deals?

    Property #1: _____

    Property #2: _____

If you think you have a great deal after you've done your analysis, but you aren't *sure*, you can always do this: First, contact a real estate agent and get his or her opinion. Second, contract and hire a referred appraiser, who charges from $150 to $500 to do an appraisal on the property.

Contracts

The biggest roadblock that keeps people from getting started and being successful in real estate investing, at least in their minds, is contracts.

They get excited about property itself, then trip up over questions about which contracts to use, what if they don't present the right contract, and what if something happens—good or bad? They use all those fears and doubts, worries and wonders, as excuses for not starting to invest.

I've met investors who've found incredible deals at 60 percent under market, but who thought they didn't have the right contract, so they let the deal slip away. Don't let this happen to you.

I'm an attorney. In law school, and after, I spent a lot of time studying contract law. I have dozens of contracts: lease-options, contract-for-deed, buyer contracts, seller contracts, one-page contracts, 20-page contracts, even 100-page contracts. Nevertheless, I don't think about contracts much because my focus is on making money, not on paperwork. And that should be your focus, too.

If someone comes to you with a car worth $50,000 and offers it to you for $1.00, will you pass on the deal because you don't have the right contract to buy it? Of course not. In the United States, all you have to do is write on a piece of paper, "I will buy your car for $1.00, and I'll give you the dollar tomorrow." Then sign and date your new document, and you have a valid contract.

I repeat, don't worry about contracts. You'll learn my tricks of the trade, but don't use them to get hung up on paperwork. If a real estate agent tells me a seller will sell to me, but I have to use the agent's contract, I will. I'd rather use mine, including as many clauses as I can, but I won't let that keep me from making a deal.

Remember your focus: making money. That takes precedence over deciphering, analyzing, and getting overly involved with contracts. Build your team to include a real estate lawyer and title company. Let them draw up your contracts. Your job is to find good deals, help people, and make money.

The One-Page Contract

Keep things simple and only use a one-page contract. Realize that when you're dealing with motivated sellers, you're likely working with anxious people. They're having problems (that's why they're motivated sellers!), and they don't want to look through a multipage contract. Its length and legal jargon can be confusing and may give them a reason to reconsider and back out.

If you're buying a piece of property, be sure to include the following:

Contingency Clause

You only need one: *"This contract is contingent upon buyer's inspection and approval before closing."* That removes all risk. At any time before closing, you can inspect the property, say you don't like it because it's not what you thought, and get out of it. Don't write a contract on a piece of property, however, unless you think that you'll definitely close on it. This clause is just your safety net if something unexpected goes wrong.

Proper Disclosure

"I am a real estate investor. I may be reselling your property for profit. I do not represent you or your interests." This could protect you in case of legal action.

Assign Payment of Closing Costs

"Seller will pay all closing costs."

Earnest Money

If you think you have to put down earnest money, type in *"$10 earnest money,"* and stipulate who will hold it.

Assign Risk

"Seller has the risk of loss up until the date of deed." That means if there's a fire or earthquake and you're scheduled to close on the property tomorrow, you're not at risk. Instead, the sellers are at risk in case of a disaster because they still own the property.

Names and Dates

These are required in order for people to sign the contract.

Clear Title and Title Insurance

Make sure you arrange for them.

I've designed separate contracts for buying and selling. If you're interested in looking at the forms I typically use, go to www.sheminrealestate.com or call 888-302-8018.

DAY 20   Action Plan

It's Up to You to Make It Happen!

✔ Get a copy of a contract from a local real estate agent to use as a model. Read it. Make sure you understand it.

✔ Get your contract ready. Have it reviewed by a local real estate attorney.

✔ Write out *by hand* between 10 and 20 copies of your contract so that you're familiar with it. Then you'll be prepared to use it the minute you find that motivated seller.

Making Offers, Part 1

Y ou've been calling about deals and talking to people. Now it's time to make some offers. Say you've found a motivated seller—shoot out an offer 30 to 40 percent below the property's market value, whatever you feel would be a great deal. Sign the contract, date it, and send it out via fax or mail. This is the beginning of a new habit. Get used to sending out signed contracts.

Before you send any offers out, have a local real estate attorney review your contract. Laws are different in every city and state. You need to fully understand all the clauses in your contract and have them reviewed by a professional.

Earnest Money

Do you have to include earnest money or a deposit on your contracts? My attorneys tell me that in order for a contract to be valid, it has to have two parties, a meeting of the minds (an agreement), and valuable consideration.

Say you write a contract to buy a house for $1,000. Then you don't need earnest money because the purchase price is the promise of valuable consideration. Your local attorney or real estate experts however, might say that you need to put earnest money down or they might require a deposit to be held in an escrow account through a title company or an attorney.

Are Contracts Assignable?

Please check with your own attorney, but my attorney tells me that all contracts in the United States are assignable (that is, you can sell them or trade them) unless they say they're not. If you'd feel more comfortable, you can include a statement in your contract, saying, "This contract is assignable."

This means that if you have a contract to buy a house for $100,000, and the house is worth $150,000, you can assign, or sell, your contract for $10,000 to another investor. That investor now steps into your shoes. He has any rights that you had under that contract, including the ability to buy the house for $100,000. He gave you $10,000 for the right to do it.

DAY 21   Action Plan

It's Up to You to Make It Happen!

✔ Shoot out five low offers.

What properties?

_____

_____

_____

_____

_____

How much did you offer for each?

_____

_____

_____

_____

_____

What was the response you received for each?

_____

_____

_____

_____

_____

Understand that if you're shooting out low offers, you may not get a response at all. But if you shoot out enough offers, it's guaranteed that *something* will happen.

Making Offers, Part 2

Today, send out 10 offers. You should need only a few minutes to send each one out, and no more than 30 to 60 minutes to send all 10. You can type the details into your computer, fill in the blanks, print them, and send them out.

One way to find motivated sellers is to send out a lot of offers. Even if you haven't talked to the people involved, you can send offers from newspaper ads, For Sale signs, and For Rent signs. If the sellers respond, they just might be motivated and be ready to sell to you!

DAY 22 Action Plan

It's Up to You to Make It Happen!

✔ Send out 10 more offers and record them here.

What properties?

_____

_____

_____

_____

_____

_____

_____

_____

_____

How much did you offer for each?

_____

_____

_____

_____

_____

_____

_____

_____

_____

What was the response you received for each?

_____

_____

_____

_____

_____

_____

_____

_____

_____

_____

Making Offers, Part 3

A man in my town, Hal, makes more money in real estate than I do. Why? He makes more offers. It's that simple. If you never make an offer on a piece of property, you won't get any. I know, because I spent my first year in real estate looking at a lot of property and doing a lot of analyses. I never made one offer, and my business went nowhere. Today, I have no qualms about sending out multiple offers each week, nor should you. If you send out enough offers, something will happen.

Are any of your offers getting accepted? The best way to get your offers accepted is to talk to the motivated seller, negotiate, and get the deal done verbally. Then, write up the contract.

Halftime Check-In

You're more than halfway through this 40-day program. I suspect you're probably not doing all the activities included in the book because people never do 100 percent of what they want to do. But imagine for just a moment what would happen if you actually did follow these action plans for two hours a day up until now. Imagine what you'd be learning, the people you'd be meeting, the networks you'd be building, the information you'd be gathering. You'd be well on your way to success in your real estate investing career!

At this point, reanalyze your commitment. Are you really committed? Are you doing the activities you need to be doing? Are you thinking and worrying too much? Or are you just enjoying reading this book so much that you've been too busy to actually execute any of these well-intentioned plans?

It's up to you to make it happen.

DAY 23   Action Plan

It's Up to You to Make It Happen!

✔ What is your commitment to your business today? Are you doing the activities? Yes or No

✔ How many offers have you sent out? _____

✔ How many offers do you think you should be sending out?

Each week _____   Each month _____   Each quarter _____

✔ What has your response rate been? _____

✔ How many of your offers are getting accepted? _____

✔ Are you making any money yet? How much? _____

✔ How could you find more properties to make offers on? List your ideas here:

_____

_____

_____

_____

✔ How many phone calls have you made to follow up on your offers? _____

✔ Send out 10 more offers. List the properties, prices, and responses here.

What properties?

_____

_____

_____

_____

_____

_____

_____

_____

_____

How much was offered for each?

_____

_____

_____

_____

_____

_____

_____

_____

_____

What responses were received?

_____

_____

_____

_____

_____

_____

_____

_____

_____

_____

Protecting Yourself

What if people try to lie to you, cheat on you, or steal from you? What if they sign a contract, then won't sell the property to you because they have already sold it to someone else? Spend your two hours on Day 24 concentrating on ways to protect yourself and your real estate business.

Stay Comfortable

The number one way to protect yourself and your business is to feel comfortable with the people you're doing business with. If you don't feel comfortable with people or don't trust them, be cautious about doing business with them. Life is too short. Why should you do business with someone you don't trust when you can spend your time doing business with people you do feel comfortable with?

Put Everything in Writing

Put every one of your contracts in writing. Your agreements with your team members also need to be in writing. Specify how you're going to get paid, how you're going to pay people, and so on. Everything you agree to do should be in writing, from the simplest transactions to the most complicated.

Record Your Contracts

When sellers sign a contract, they're motivated. If they're highly motivated, they might be under emotional and financial stress. Someone could come along two days later, offer them more, and that person could sign a contract with them. If they sell the property to that person, then you're out, even though you have a signed contract. It can happen. It's happened to me.

One way to protect yourself is to contact your local title or real estate attorney, or with your local registrar of deeds, and have that person record a copy of your contract. This is also called an affidavit, a legal term for letter. This letter would say something like this: "I have Mrs. Smith's property under contract for $100,000 and I'm going to close August 31."

Recording the contract with the registrar of deeds puts the world on notice that you have an interest in the property. So, if the seller tries to sell it to someone else, you have already recorded it and they cannot pass on a good title without dealing with your interest in the property.

I do this on every property I feel the seller might sell to someone else. You may want to do it on all your properties. After you have been in real estate long enough and have dealt with enough motivated sellers, one of them is likely to try to sell his or her property to someone else after you have put it under contract.

Should You Incorporate?

Probably. Most attorneys and accountants recommend that real estate investors open a Limited Liability Company, which is a type of corporation. There are also C-corporations, S-corporations, partnerships, limited partnerships, and sole proprietorships. Remember, whatever business you're involved in and whatever structure you choose, you're responsible for your activities, and you could get sued for what you're doing.

If a lawsuit is filed against you and everything you own is in your own name, your personal assets (e.g., home, car) as well as your business properties could be lost in a judgment against you. In the eyes of the law, a properly created and maintained corporation is a separate person. So, if some of your real estate is in a Limited Liability Company or a contract is in the name of the LLC, your losses are limited to the assets that come under the umbrella of your LLC.

Remember, a corporation doing business must have proper insurance. Please check with your insurance agent to make sure your LLC is properly insured for the activities you're doing.

Should you handle your insurance yourself? A few years ago, I had knee surgery. I simply had to have some cartilage taken out; I could probably have done it myself. Would you feel comfortable doing knee surgery on yourself? I doubt it. Doing your own legal work can be considered equivalent to doing your own medical work.

When I have a medical operation, I want a professionally trained doctor who's specifically trained in the procedure and has performed the operation many times. With legal work, there are many details and changes in the law to take into consideration. That's why you want a good, qualified attorney to make sure the corporation is properly set up and maintained.

Once they set it up, attorneys will instruct you how to sign your documents with the correct corporation name. They will also keep you up to date on the annual paperwork required to keep it valid.

People who want to save a few hundred dollars by doing their own corporations often don't have the proper operating agreements; they don't have the proper filings; and they don't conduct the proper meeting every year and show the proper minutes. In other words, they don't keep their corporate book in order. Then, if they faced a lawsuit, a good lawyer will ask them to present these things that they don't have. The judge will say the corporation is invalid, leaving the people who wanted to save a few hundred dollars with no protection.

I highly recommend hiring an attorney as one of your team members to protect you.

It's important to meet with your accountant as well as your attorney when deciding on corporations because the tax implications vary for each of these entities. Do you want to be taxed as an individual, as a partnership, as a corporation?

I suggest you meet with a qualified accountant to determine which one would be best for you in your particular circumstances.

Pre-Paid Legal Services

I've saved a lot of money on legal fees by using a national company called Pre-Paid Legal Services. It's a 30-year-old company that's traded on the NYSE and ranked highly by financial magazines. Pre-Paid Legal Services does for legal bills what medical insurance does for medical bills. For $26 to $50 a month, you gain access to great attorneys across the country. Once you become a member, they never raise your rates, *unlike* medical insurance. Working with Pre-Paid Legal Services, your spouse and children (up to ages 18 to 23, depending on whether or not they're in college) will also be covered.

I'm an independent associate with Pre-Paid Legal, and also a happy member. If you're interested in finding out more about this company, please go to my web site at www.prepaidlegal.com\info\Shemin. There you can see the different kinds of memberships offered and sign up if you find what's right for you. The company requires a month-to-month contract, so you're not obligated long-term to this insurance. I highly recommend you try it, use it, and keep it.

Briefly, here's what Pre-Paid Legal Services offers:

Legal Consultation and Advice

- As real estate investor, you'll have questions—about contracts, real estate law, even personal questions. Any time you have a legal question, you can call your Pre-Paid Legal Services attorney and get answers.

- Professionals in affiliated law firms will make calls and write letters on your behalf. You'll receive unlimited legal service for personal matters and a few services for business matters.

- Ask Pre-Paid Legal Services to review contracts or documents before you sign them.

Comprehensive Will

About 70 percent of Americans do not have a will. A good will drafted by a top law firm will cost you from $200 to $1,000. That's included at no additional cost to you once you're a member. In fact, it's the first thing Pre-Paid Legal Services will do for you. Their lawyers will also review your will once a year to make sure it reflects changes in your life. Please get a will today; you don't want your state's legal system to determine how your property will be dispersed at your death.

Traffic Representation

After a 15-day waiting period from the date you join, you will have representation from Pre-Paid Legal Services if you get a speeding ticket or any other moving violations. If you are criminally charged (for instance, with manslaughter or vehicular homicide), your car insurance won't pay for your defense but Pre-Paid Legal will. Assuming you weren't on drugs or alcohol when the accident happened, this service provides unlimited defense.

Legal Defense

- During the first year of membership, you're eligible for 50 hours of legal defense, which will increase to more than 200 hours a year.
- The IRS audit defense covers up to 50 hours. You can also call and ask legal tax questions. Remember, if you work in real estate investing, you're in a high-audit category.
- Any legal services not fully covered are still available from Pre-Paid Legal Services at a discounted rate with your membership.

Legal Shield

Joining Pre-Paid Legal Services gives you access to legal representation 24 hours a day. (If you have teenagers who drive, you need to have this coverage.)

Credit Identity Theft Protection

For an extra $9.95 a month, Pre-Paid Legal Services (in conjunction with Kroll) will protect your credit and send you an e-mail anytime your credit is checked, or take action if someone takes your social security number and abuses it. Identity theft is the most common crime going today. Don't become a victim of it. Get protection for only a few dollars a month with one of the best companies in the country.

Go to my web site at www.prepaidlegal.com\info\Shemin to sign up for Pre-Paid Legal Services. I've used their services for years and have been extremely pleased. Many of my students have saved thousands and thousands of dollars by turning to the lawyers at Pre-Paid Legal Services.

DAY 24   Action Plan

It's Up to You to Make It Happen!

✔ Are you comfortable with the people you're doing business with? Yes or No

✔ Is there anyone you need to stop working with? Name the individuals here:

_____

_____

_____

_____

✔ Have you put your agreements with members of your team in writing? If not, take care of that today.

✔ Find the registrar of deeds in your community and learn how to record a contract so that you're ready when the time to deliver a contract comes.

✔ Spend Day 24 considering whether it's time to incorporate. Meet with a trained professional to determine the best entity for your business (for instance, corporation, sub-chapter S corporation, LLC, etc.). If you own rental property, consider establishing another LLC for the management of the property, which is separate from the ownership. If you have other businesses or wealth, consider segregating those assets and activities as well. Meet with your attorney and accountant to find out which entities and taxation systems are best for your situation.

✔ If you're interested in finding out more about Pre-Paid Legal Services and becoming a member, go to my web site at www.prepaidlegal.com\info\Shemin and sign up.

Financing Options, Part 1

When you find a property, what will you do with it? Many people want to go the traditional route and buy the piece of property. I highly recommend that beginners start with wholesaling and lease optioning properties they find. But if you buy property, you'll want to finance it. So on Day 25, start to build your ability to finance and buy properties.

Ways to Finance Property

Use Your Own Cash

You may have lots of cash. You may have done well in the stock market, sold a house, or accumulated wealth in business. Whatever your situation, I recommend that you not use your own cash. Why use your cash when you don't have to? Why put it at risk?

Even though you'll learn ways to purchase property without using any of your own cash or credit, many of you will still make that choice. That's okay. I've done it, and I don't see anything wrong with it. But if you're out there finding a lot of deals and using your own cash or credit, you'll eventually run out of it. Why put your own cash or credit at risk? Learn how to run your business with O.P.M. (other people's money).

Use Your Own Credit

You may have excellent credit and be able to get a good mortgage from a bank. If that's true, congratulations. However, I suggest you avoid using your own credit to buy property because you have other choices.

Use the Existing Mortgage

The best source for cash or funding for a property is the one that's already there—that is, the mortgage. Most properties already carry a mortgage.

Traditionally in real estate, when you buy a house, you sell your house first to pay off your mortgage. Then you buy someone else's house, get a new mortgage, and put your mortgage into that house. Meanwhile, they sell their house, pay off their mortgage, buy another house, and get a new mortgage. Essentially what has occurred? A series of transferred mortgages. It's like musical chairs; the banks moved the mortgages around and charged a whole lot of fees to do so.

I think the best mortgage to have is the one that's already on the property you want to buy. And if there's no mortgage on the property, it's even better because the people might let you do owner's terms and make the monthly payments directly to them. This arrangement is commonly referred to in these ways: "seller's financing," "owner's terms," "taking over a mortgage," or "contract for deed."

You and your local real estate attorney or title company will come up with the best technical solution to finance a property. Let the professionals draw up the proper paperwork. But while you're learning the different technical terms, don't get hung up on them. Your job is to focus on finding deals and making money.

> When I buy a property, I always try to get the property in my name. If the deed remains in the sellers' names and something bad happens (for instance, the IRS places a lien against them, the couple gets divorced, or they're sued), all of the sudden the title to the house could be in jeopardy. I'd prefer to have the title in my name and so should you.

Let's assume you want to buy the house and take over payments. Your escrow company can typically handle this in two different ways:

1. *Get the deed put in your name*, so that now you own the house and have to pay the mortgage.

2. *Keep the deed in the seller's name* and execute a contract for deed, which says you've entered into a contract and will make specified payments each month. When you fulfill all your obligations and make all the payments you've agreed to make, you get to have the deed. This is commonly referred to as "getting owner's terms."

For example, let's take a house worth $100,000 that has a $70,000 outstanding mortgage on it. They sellers are willing to sell it to you for $75,000. You could take over their payments ($600 a month) on the $70,000 mortgage. You'd then have to come up with $5,000 (the difference between the sales price and the mortgage). So you could use your cash or someone else's cash, or you could give them a note for $5,000 against the property. It would become a second mortgage that you could pay off over time—maybe over 1 year, 5 years, or even 20 years. It would depend on how good a negotiator you are and how motivated the sellers are—how much they need that $5,000 in cash.

Identity Package

Why would people let you take over their mortgage? Well, they won't be willing if they don't trust you. So I highly recommend that you create an identity package that helps give you credibility as an investor.

How do you do this? Assemble a nice folder from your local print shop or office store that includes your picture, resume, background, recommendations from your Boy Scout leader, friends, boss, people you've done business with, and testimonials from people you've helped in real estate. Take pictures of the houses you're working on and include them. If you have good credit, you might want to include a copy of your credit report. Your identity package enables you to point out that you have great credit, that you do what you say you'll do, and that you have a track record of making the payments. Include anything that will increase trust in you and put people's minds at ease about your credibility.

When you're out doing real estate, you can show prospective sellers your business and personal information. They'll have a bit more trust in you because you'll present yourself as a professional.

Other businesses have identity packages. I recommend you spend time and money creating a highly professional one.

DAY 25   Action Plan

It's Up to You to Make It Happen!

✔ On Day 25, start putting your identity package together. Check off each component when it's completed. Your identity package should include the following items:

Item	Completed
Your picture	_____
Resume	_____
Background summary	_____
Recommendations	_____
Testimonials	_____
Pictures of houses you've worked on	_____
Credit report, if it's good	_____
Other items to build your client's trust	_____

Financing Options, Part 2

When homeowners let you take over their mortgage, how can they buy another house? After all, their names are still on the old mortgage. Their credit report will still show them having to pay the old mortgage. But if your title company produces a contract that shows you will pay the mortgage amount each month, the seller of the property can qualify for a new mortgage by showing the lender this contract. Both you and the seller are covered.

More Ways to Finance Property

Use Someone Else's Cash or Credit

Whether you have money or credit or not, another way to finance properties is to find someone who does. Consider approaching three to four partners who might be interested in investing in real estate but don't have as much time, energy, or knowledge as you do.

Today, most everyone wants to invest in real estate. A lot of people have lost money in the stock market in the last 5 to 10 years and have now become interested in real estate. So develop a business plan to include in your identity package. Show them that plan and your activity list. Go to three to four people and ask, "If I find a deal, would you like to use your credit, not even your money, to get the deal? Then we'll split the profits and set up a win-win situation."

Do you know anyone who might be interested in this type of partnership? Do you think you can find three or four people who'd be interested in working with you in this way?

Start contacting three to four potential money partners. You can go back to your original business team to see if any of the members want to become your money partners. Another place to look is at your local real estate association. You'll meet people there who might want to consider investing in some of your deals—if you approach them the right way. They may even want to buy some of your deals.

Use Hard Moneylenders

Another way to buy a property without using your own money is to work with hard moneylenders. Find them; they're in your area. They advertise in your newspapers, and your mortgage brokers might know of them.

They are people who make special real estate loans. They lend from 60 percent to 75 percent of the loan-to-value on a property. They're not concerned with your credit rating; they're more interested in the value of the property, which they use as collateral. They can close quickly, but they charge more points and higher interest than traditional financing through a bank or mortgage company. For instance, many hard moneylenders charge from 2 to 10 points, and from 11 percent to 15 percent in interest. Their prices vary from region to region of the country, depending on the strength of the market.

Remember, these are the lenders of last resort. They charge more points and interest, but they can quickly and easily make decisions. They won't look at your credit in the same way a bank or mortgage company does, which can work in your favor.

Business Plan

On Day 26, start to write a very simple business plan that's one to four pages long. You can use that business plan to show potential money partners the activities you'll be doing. Assure them that they'll have a first mortgage on the properties, secured by the properties themselves, and that you'll only be buying deals that are 20 percent to 30 percent below market. That investor would be fairly safe if you're following the systems laid out here, as well as running comparable sales and getting market verifications.

DAY 26 Action Plan

It's Up to You to Make It Happen!

✔ Your homework for today is to find two hard moneylenders who are actively involved in lending people money. You also want to meet these people because they're excellent sources for finding motivated sellers and buyers, as well as for lending money. Again, everything is negotiable. Ask them what they want. Don't assume anything; ask them upfront.

Hard Moneylenders:

Name: _____   Phone Number: _____

Name: _____   Phone Number: _____

✔ It's time to draw up your business plan; make it from one to four pages long. Include it in your identity package.

✔ Whom would you like to contact to be your money partners? List them here.

Money Partners:

Name: _____   Phone Number: _____

Name: _____   Phone Number: _____

Name: _____   Phone Number: _____

Name: _____   Phone Number: _____

Your Financial Statement

You might think you don't have enough money or credit to buy property or get a loan right now. But you might be surprised; there are a multitude of loan programs available to real estate investors. Why not get preapproved for a loan to see what you could afford to buy? If you are successful, you would have funds available just in case.

You should look into having funds available for several reasons:

- To be preapproved so you can quickly buy the right property that comes along
- To start networking with mortgage brokers and hard moneylenders
- To take a financial picture of where you are now (after you get involved in real estate investing, this picture will look better and better)
- To make you aware of your own financial and credit situation and start to take remedial action if necessary

Once you know your credit status, contact your attorney at PrePaidLegal .com\info\Shemin if you find discrepancies or problems. Alternatively, you

Be aware of the difference in meaning between "prequalifying" and "getting preapproved" to borrow money from traditional lenders like banks and mortgage companies. Prequalifying doesn't mean much. It just means, based on your income, they think you can buy a home up to a certain price, or handle a certain mortgage payment a month. Preapproval means you've gone to a banker or mortgage broker who has pulled your credit and verified your income, so that you're ready to take on a loan. All that you'll need to complete the transaction is a sales contract on a property and perhaps an appraisal. So get preapproved rather than prequalified. Preapproval has a much more substantial value.

can learn how to do credit repair yourself and start fixing it. I recommend that you get a copy of your credit report at least every six months (definitely once a year) to make sure that no potential problems are lurking there. Almost half of all credit reports have some type of mistake in them.

DAY 27 Action Plan

It's Up to You to Make It Happen!

✔ Fill out a financial statement from your bank or accountant, so that you know exactly where you are in terms of financial assets and liabilities.

✔ Contact one good mortgage broker and one hard moneylender and apply for a loan just in case. Network with the mortgage broker and hard moneylender. See if they have any deals or know anyone who is looking to buy property. List the people you contacted here:

_____

_____

_____

_____

Wholesaling, Part 1

Here's a quick description of wholesaling: First you put a property under contract, then you sell it to somebody else before you have to close. Have you bought it yet? No. Have you borrowed money yet? No. You haven't used any cash or credit. You've put it under contract, having from 30 to 90 days to close (whatever you agreed to), and you have a contingency clause in the contract, so you have a way out if it doesn't work for you (so you have very little risk). Now you control the property. You can sell it (wholesale it) or perhaps buy it yourself.

You may want to include the following phrase in your contract to make you feel more comfortable: "I may resell this property for a profit. I can assign the contract." Then you've disclosed what you plan to do in writing.

The minute you've found the motivated seller, done your analysis, negotiated, and put the property under contract, then turn around and sell it before you have to close. In this way, you're wholesaling to other investors and other buyers. Everything in this country has a retail market—where people buy and sell at full price—and a wholesale market—where people buy and sell at discount. Real estate also has a wholesale market. In addition to becoming a real estate doctor, you can be a real estate wholesaler.

Walk through a Wholesale Deal

Here's an example of a wholesale deal. You find a house worth $200,000, with no repairs needed. You get it under contract for $140,000 and have 45 days to close on the sale. You have the right to buy the house for $140,000. The day the seller signs the contract, you run an ad in the paper, "Investment special. Great house. Won't last. Call now."

Say you get 20 calls from the ad. You have comps in your folder, so you can fax over the comps to the callers. Also include the opinions of what it's worth from your market professional, and the contractor's bid—now you look like a real professional. Tell your callers to drive by the house (and not to disturb the tenants), and call you back if they're interested in buying it. Tell them to go by right away because it's going to sell very quickly. Always tell them you plan to have it sold within three business days. Give them a sense of urgency.

Suppose one caller drives by the house and calls you back, saying, "I buy houses over there all the time, and I wouldn't pay more than $100,000 for it." The second person calls and says she buys over there all the time and never pays more than $95,000. You've just learned you may not have a good deal. Or maybe their information is incorrect. In your business, you're always gathering information. If you've done your homework correctly and followed the system, the house *is* worth $200,000. Suppose other investors drive by, call you, and say, "That house is worth $200,000; I'd pay $180,000 for it."

If someone says she'll pay $180,000, what do you do next? If you sell it to that person immediately, you'll make $40,000. However, you'd be forgetting one of these action-plan principles: ABN (always be negotiating). Here, you're doing reverse negotiating because you're the seller. Tell the person, "I want you to have a good deal. I want you to make money, but what's the most you could pay for this property and be okay?" She might say, "Well, the appraisal is at $200,000 and I think it's actually worth $210,000, but I tell you what, I couldn't pay you a penny over $185,000." How much more money would you have made, just by asking one question? $5,000! Maybe they know something you don't know; maybe the house is worth $250,000. Remember, the only thing that will tell you what a house is actually worth is what someone is willing to pay for it.

Then you go back to negotiating, "Can you do any better, can you do any better, can you pay a little more?"

"No I can't. $185,000 is it."

"I was thinking $193,817."

"No, $185,000."

If you agree, next you sign a contract to sell the property at $185,000. Now, you're a seller. You give your contract to buy this house for $140,000 and your contract to sell it for $185,000 to your title company. They do all the paperwork for closing, and you pick up the check for the difference.

The one thing that will determine if you'll be able to sell your wholesale properties is whether you've found a good deal. If it's a good deal, someone will buy it for more than you put it under contract for. If it's not a good deal, you may not be able to sell it.

DAY 28   Action Plan

It's Up to You to Make It Happen!

✔ For Day 28, focus on building your buyers list. How do you find buyers of property? You can always run an ad like this:

**Possible investment properties.
Must be preapproved
or have cash. Call now.**

If you've been doing the activities we've been talking about—calling the I Buy Houses ads, going to the auctions, going to the real estate association meetings, having lunch with different investors, meeting with your mortgage brokers and bankers and real estate agents—you should already have begun building a list of buyers. That is one of your most important databases. Always add to and fine-tune this all-important list.

Buyers List

Name: _____

Address: _____

Phone number: _____

Fax number: _____

E-mail address: _____

Type of property looking for (buy, fix up, and sell; hold and rent; wholesale):

_____

How many properties do you want to buy? _____

What areas do you want to buy in? _____

Name: _____

Address: _____

Phone number: _____

Fax number: _____

E-mail address: _____

Type of property looking for (buy, fix up, and sell; hold and rent; wholesale):

_____

How many properties do you want to buy? _____

What areas do you want to buy in? _____

Name: _____

Address: _____

Phone number: _____

Fax number: _____

E-mail address: _____

Type of property looking for (buy, fix up, and sell; hold and rent; wholesale):

_____

How many properties do you want to buy? _____

What areas do you want to buy in? _____

Name: _____

Address: _____

Phone number: _____

Fax number: _____

E-mail address: _____

Type of property looking for (buy, fix up, and sell; hold and rent; wholesale):

_____

How many properties do you want to buy? _____

What areas do you want to buy in? _____

Name: _____

Address:_____

Phone number: _____

Fax number: _____

E-mail address: _____

Type of property looking for (buy, fix up, and sell; hold and rent; wholesale):

_____

How many properties do you want to buy? _____

What areas do you want to buy in? _____

Wholesaling, Part I

Name: _____

Address: _____

Phone number: _____

Fax number: _____

E-mail address: _____

Type of property looking for (buy, fix up, and sell; hold and rent; wholesale):

_____

How many properties do you want to buy? _____

What areas do you want to buy in? _____

Wholesaling, Part 2

It's time to start thinking about doing a reverse wholesale deal. Here's how it works. Call your buyers, and ask what kind of property they're looking for. Until now, you've been looking for a motivated seller, analyzing the selected property, and putting it under contract. You can also do a reverse wholesale deal, which means you find the buyer first.

One buyer might say he'd like to buy houses to fix up and sell in one particular area. Write that information down. With your two hours today, look for a house that fits his criteria. You've found your buyer first; now go out and find the property.

Call three to five other wholesalers (people you've been contacting through the newspaper ads, I Buy Houses ads, lease-optioning ads, meetings at your real estate association, and so forth). Ask what they're looking for. Do they have more property than buyers? Do they have more buyers than property? What do they need? They may know people who will buy any rehab (a house that you can buy, fix up, and sell) right now; they may know people who will buy any good piece of rental property that will generate cash flow.

When I was starting out in real estate, a gentleman in my town, Tom, heard I was buying duplexes. Back then, one could buy nice brick duplexes in a certain part of Nashville for about $60,000 to $70,000. They were worth $90,000 to $100,000. He drove me around, pointing out a few duplexes and asking what I'd pay for each.

He pointed to one and said, "Robert, see that duplex over there? What would you pay for that?" I told him, "That's a nice duplex. I'd pay at least $60,000 for that." He pointed out another one, "Robert, what would you pay for that one?" "That's a really nice one, even better than the last. I'd probably pay $65,000 for that because it would be worth $90,000 at least."

Tom dropped me off, drove back to the duplexes, banged on the doors, and asked the tenants who owned or managed the properties. He called the owners/managers and asked what they'd sell the duplexes for. They knew what they were worth, but had bought them inexpensively many years ago, so they let him have them for $55,000 each. Tom negotiated and put them under contract for $54,000, called me up a day or two later, and said, "Remember that duplex that you said you'd pay $60,000 for? Could you do a little better?" I went up to $62,000. He wholesaled a bunch of duplexes by finding the buyer first (me), then purchasing the property.

I know four other investors in my town with whom I've completed more than 100 deals in the last four years. They're serious, they understand the business, and they have funds and partners. You too need to meet dedicated investors like these.

DAY 29   Action Plan

It's Up to You to Make It Happen!

✔ Homework: Call some of the potential buyers from your list, find out what they're looking for, spend two hours, and see if you can find something your buyers might want.

Buyer: _____   Property looking for: _____

Buyer: _____   Property looking for: _____

Buyer: _____   Property looking for: _____

Buyer: _____   Property looking for: _____

Buyer: _____   Property looking for: _____

Buyer: _____   Property looking for: _____

Buyer: _____   Property looking for: _____

Buyer: _____   Property looking for: _____

Buyer: _____   Property looking for: _____

Buyer: _____   Property looking for: _____

Buyer: _____   Property looking for: _____

Buyer: _____   Property looking for: _____

Buyer: _____   Property looking for: _____

Buyer: _____   Property looking for: _____

Buyer: _____   Property looking for: _____

Wholesaling, Part 3

No matter which way you choose to close a wholesale deal, who controls the closing? The answer is simple: your referred, respected real estate attorney or title company contact who advises you on the best way to close each deal. Let the professional tell you which method is the best. Your job is to find a deal, analyze it, put it under contract, make sure people are making money, and go to the closing. Here are examples of these types of closings:

- Double closing
- Collapsed closing
- Assignment of contract

Double Closing

You buy the house from Susie Seller for $200,000 and sell it to Bill Buyer for $220,000. Bill brings his $220,000 to closing at 3:00 P.M. The escrow company takes his $220,000 and gives $200,000 to Susie, because that's what she wanted. Bill signs a closing statement saying he's buying the house from you for $220,000. Immediately, the escrow company representative goes in the next room, gives Susie her $200,000, and she signs the contract saying she's selling the house to you for $200,000. There's a $20,000 difference. You can put that in your pocket. That's called a double or simultaneous closing.

It's important that you disclose in writing to both the seller and the buyer exactly what you're doing. Please meet with your own local attorney and put this disclosure in your contract. You have to disclose what you're doing in writing to protect yourself because, basically, you're selling something you don't own—yet.

Collapsed Closing

Bill Buyer brings in his $220,000. The lawyer takes it and gives $200,000 to Susie Seller. One deed gets transferred from Susie to Bill. There's also one closing statement. The back of the statement reads, "Assignment fee (or wholesale fee, consulting fee, finder's fee, or marketing fee) of $20,000 to (your name)." That comes out of the closing statement.

Assignment of Contract

This is probably the best and cleanest way to close a deal. You tell the end buyer, Bill Buyer, "I have the right to buy Susie Seller's house for $200,000—here's the contract. I will sell you my contract (not the property). I'll sell you the *right* to buy the house for $20,000. So at closing, when you bring in $220,000, then $20,000 goes to me. The title company will assign my contract to you for $20,000, and you give $200,000 to Susie Seller. She's happy because that's what she wanted, you're happy because you have a new home, and I'm happy because I helped two families and made some money."

When you sell a contract, you're basically selling your right to the property and the person who buys it from you steps into your shoes.

Although assignment of contract is the cleanest way to wholesale property, you can encounter problems. Specifically, all the people involved (including the real estate agents) know how much you're making on the deal. And no matter how much money they may be making themselves, other people in real estate don't like you to make money. When you're doing a double closing, however, they have no idea how much you're being paid.

To avoid this problem, a lot of wholesalers wholesale through a land trust. They transfer the property or the contract into a land trust, which is often named after the address of the property, for example, 100 Jones Street Land Trust. This arrangement gives them a measure of anonymity. So no one knows who is profiting from the sale or how much money is coming his way.

Marketing the Property

Let's say you've found a good deal and put it under contract. When do you take action? Immediately. Even though you have 30 to 90 days to close, start looking for your buyer right away. Run an ad, contact people on your buyers list, hand out flyers around the neighborhood, call lots of real estate agents—see if anyone will buy the property.

If a week goes by and no one shows interest, you've gathered information that something's wrong. Go back to the original seller, and use your contingency clause to get out of the contract. Don't wait until the twenty-ninth day of the contract to say you have a problem. You've already disclosed that you might resell it; you've got a contingency clause in place. You simply can't do the deal. Don't wait until the last minute and risk painting yourself into a corner.

Guess what? The reverse problem can also happen. You thought the property was worth $280,000 and had it under contract for $200,000. After calling real estate agents and buyers, you discover that the house is really worth $300,000. That's a nice problem to have, and it's happened to me more often than the first scenario.

The point is to start marketing immediately. Fax, phone, and e-mail your buyers list; run ads; get permission to put a sign in the yard—don't use just one method to sell a property; use multiple streams. Get real estate agents involved; pay them a commission if they bring a buyer who is preapproved. Go to your real estate association. Hand

> Between 50 percent and 60 percent of all properties are sold off a sign in the yard. In fact, most people use a standard real estate sign. When I sell a property, I use an 8-foot or 12-foot or 20-foot sign that can be seen by anybody driving down the road at 80 miles an hour with one eye closed. I put streamers on it and hand out flyers to everyone in the neighborhood. Be sure to get permission and alert the sellers that you're marketing the property because you don't want them to be surprised. Sometimes you won't get permission; in those cases, you really have to work your buyers list.

out flyers to everybody, with the following printed on them: "Urgent. Won't last. Must sell by the end of the week." Again, if the numbers are right and the deal is good, it will sell. If it's not a good deal, it won't sell.

Offering financing will also help sell a property, so go to your hard moneylenders, and ask how much they'd lend on the property. After you do that, you can tell your buyers you already have financing in place. Maybe you have a partner who's willing to put up 75 percent to 80 percent of the purchase price of the property in return for 11 percent paid in interest. Maybe you've negotiated owner's terms on the deal with the seller. You can pass that cost on to your buyer.

Life is too short. There's too much business out there. I'd rather walk away and go on to the next three deals than have people complaining and upset at me—whether they're right or wrong. I would rather be happy than right.

We have a saying in Tennessee: Pigs get fat, hogs get slaughtered. To me, that means there's enough business out there for everyone, so don't be greedy. Sometimes, it's best in a relationship or business transaction that's not working to just smile and walk away, even if you have contracts and disclosures. You have to make your own business decision and do what you think is good business—whatever is ethical and makes you feel good.

> One of my business policies and procedures is never to get involved in any transaction in which people are not absolutely happy and satisfied. I've walked away from a few deals that would have brought me high earnings because the people were, in my view, irrational and illogical, upset and unhappy. I was happy to walk away.

DAY 30 Action Plan

It's Up to You to Make It Happen!

Continue wholesaling to other wholesalers. Ask what they need, find out what they want. Go out and get it. Other wholesalers and investors will become some of your best clients and your best friends.

✔ Today, find three to five wholesalers, call them—maybe take them to lunch—and find out what they need, so that you can look for it, using the systems you've already learned.

Buyer: _____ Property looking for: _____

Buyer: _____ Property looking for: _____

Buyer: _____ Property looking for: _____

Buyer: _____ Property looking for: _____

Buyer: _____ Property looking for: _____

Lease Optioning, Part 1

Lease optioning is a great way to make money investing in real estate. And if you're renting your home, you might want to consider lease optioning to stop throwing all your rent dollars away.

How a Lease Option Works

Lease It

You lease a property for a set amount of time, from 1 to 20 years, for example. The longer, the better—for you. Lease it at the lowest rent rate that you can possibly get.

Option It

Get an option to buy the property at below what the market value is, if possible. That gives you an option to buy it. However, you're not *obligated* to buy it. If the market goes up, you can exercise your option to buy it and make a lot of money. If the market goes down, you can walk away.

Turn It Around

Once you lease a property with an option to buy it, you can turn around and rent-to-own it (or lease option it) to someone else for an even higher monthly payment.

So, if you've lease optioned it for $1,000 a month and the market rent is $1,400, you can turn around and lease it for $1,400 and make $400 a month. If your option price to buy the property is $150,000 and the property is worth $180,000, at any time, you can sell it to someone for $180,000, exercise or use your option for $150,000, go to closing, and pick up your check for the difference of $30,000.

Lease optioning is an excellent way to control property without all the borrowing or using credit. You can lease option the house you live in, a vacation home, or investment property. Also, when you lease option, part of the rent payment goes toward the purchase price every month. If you're paying $1,000 a month, you could perhaps negotiate $200 to $300 a month of that going toward the purchase price. So in a year, if you decide to buy it, you have $300 × 12 = $3,600 credit toward the purchase price, which might cover your down payment and/or closing costs. It's an excellent way to stop throwing your rent dollars away.

Offer Your Program

To start building your lease optioning business, follow up For Rent ads, using the systems discussed earlier. See if you can find motivated landlords or property managers who might want to lease option the property or perhaps even sell it to you. Run the numbers with them to point out how little they are really making.

Find out the two things the landlords don't like and address them. Usually, they don't like collecting the rent, dealing with the repairs, or sacrificing freedom. Then turn the tables on them; offer *them* an opportunity. Tell them you have a program and need to see if they qualify. Your program assures them that they will always receive their rents on time. Tell them you're a professional real estate investor and will pay their required rent on time every month. Second, they will get out of the repair business—all those little, dinky repairs that drive them crazy, the busted toilets and stopped-up sinks. Say you'll take care of those repairs for them up to the first $300 or $500, or whatever amount is appropriate.

Try to lease the property for 2, 3, 4, 5, maybe 10 years with the option to buy it. When you get your option, use your negotiating techniques to find how motivated the seller is and get as big a discount as you can.

DAY 31   Action Plan

It's Up to You to Make It Happen!

✔ Spend an hour or two calling 10 For Rent ads. You're looking for people who are interested in lease optioning their property. If you make 10 calls and no one calls you back, make 10 more, and 10 more, until you have talked to at least two or three people. Leave messages with the rest, so that you can start to build your lease-option business. Record the responses and follow up.

Contact _____ Property _____
Response _____
_____

Contact _____ Property _____
Response _____
_____

Contact _____ Property _____
Response _____
_____

Lease Optioning, Part 1

Contact _____ Property _____

Response _____

_____

Contact _____ Property _____

Response _____

_____

Contact _____ Property _____

Response _____

_____

Contact _____ Property _____

Response _____

_____

Contact _____ Property _____

Response _____

_____

Contact _____ Property _____

Response _____

_____

Contact _____ Property _____

Response _____

_____

Lease Optioning, Part 2

Remember, you've focused on solving people's problems, but you have to make sure they have a problem first. With lease optioning, you're dealing with landlords and property managers who may be tired of the day-to-day hassles of taking care of the property. On Day 32, spend time carefully qualifying your prospects and making sure they can benefit from your lease-option offers. The following questions will guide your discussion.

Ask Questions

Ask questions to learn what the landlords and property managers you contact don't like about managing rental property:

- Do they like being landlords?
- How much time do they spend managing the property?

- How much money have they spent fixing the property?

- How long has any of their properties been vacant?

- Would they be interested in a program, if they qualify, in which they could get out of business, out of the headache business?

- What would they do with their free time if they didn't have to manage their property?

Make sure you find that out.

Use the Answers to Negotiate

After you've found out what they don't like, start to negotiate. That's step number one. Go over the numbers. Point out that they're leasing it for $1,500 a month, for example, but it's been vacant, and they've spent a lot on repairs, so they're only making $1,000 a month.

Step number two is to get some of that rent as credit toward purchasing it— perhaps $200 to $400 a month.

Step number three is to negotiate the best option price, asking for as big a discount as you can get for that rent-to-own property.

DAY 32   Action Plan

It's Up to You to Make It Happen!

✔ Call 10 more For Rent ads. If you don't reach anyone, call 10 more, and 10 more, and 10 more. I believe that in a week's time, if you're serious about lease optioning, you should make up to 20 calls a day. That means within a week, you've made at least 100 calls on For Rent ads.

✔ Track the responses you're getting.

Contact _____ Property _____
Response _____
_____

Contact _____ Property _____
Response _____
_____

Contact _____ Property _____
Response _____
_____

Contact _____ Property _____
Response _____
_____

Contact _____ Property _____
Response _____
_____

Contact _____ Property _____
Response _____
_____

Contact _____ Property _____
Response _____
_____

Lease Optioning, Part 2

Contact _____ Property _____

Response _____

_____

Contact _____ Property _____

Response _____

_____

Contact _____ Property _____

Response _____

_____

Lease Optioning, Part 3

Whenever you're buying or acquiring interest in a property, take action in this order:

1. Always try to get the deed and owner's terms, even if you're going to lease option it.

2. If they won't give you the deed, then try to get a contract for the deed. That gives you some type of ownership interest.

If they won't give you either of those, ask for a lease with an option to buy. They still own the property, but you control it under this arrangement.

Things to Look Out For

On any property you lease option, protect yourself by taking care of the following issues:

- Get a title search to make sure you can get a clear title.
- If there's a mortgage on the property, verify that they're paying it.

- Make sure that on any property you have an interest in, you have insurance in your name, because you now have an insurable interest in the property.

- Be sure the taxes are paid.

So if you're lease optioning or getting owner's terms on a property, what's the best way to make sure those items are taken care of? You pay them. You pay the mortgage, taxes, and insurance. Make sure your name or corporate identity is written on all of the paperwork.

If the seller won't let you do that, then put a third party in charge of making the payments—an accountant, a banker, an attorney—someone you trust. If the seller won't allow you to do that, then let them pay it, but make sure they send you a receipt every month, so you can be certain these payments are being made. If six months go by and the payments haven't been made, then your great deal could become a bad one.

DAY 33 Action Plan

It's Up to You to Make It Happen!

✔ Again, call on 10 For Rent ads, 10 more For Rent ads, 10 more For Rent ads—up to 50 For Rent ads using your two hours, until you get a hold of a few people.

✔ Go back over your list of people you called over the last few days. Those who didn't call you back, call again. Remember, a policy and procedure I use, and you can use in your action system, is to call people every day until you get a response.

✔ Your goal is to get a signed lease, with a signed option. Then record that option.

Contact _____ Property _____

Response _____

_____

Contact _____ Property _____

Response _____

_____

Contact _____ Property _____

Response _____

_____

Contact _____ Property _____

Response _____

_____

Contact _____ Property _____

Response _____

_____

Contact _____ Property _____

Response _____

_____

Contact _____ Property _____

Response _____

_____

Lease Optioning, Part 3

Contact _____ Property _____

Response _____

_____

Contact _____ Property _____

Response _____

_____

Contact _____ Property _____

Response _____

_____

Lease Optioning, Part 4

How do you find For Rent properties to call on? By looking in the newspaper, driving for dollars, following up For Rent signs, phoning rental agencies, and talking to property managers who might be willing to work a deal (make sure they're paid their commission and management fee).

Negotiating Your Lease Option

Pay attention to these three key areas when you're negotiating a lease option:

1. Rent credit
2. Repairs
3. Down payment

Rent Credit

When negotiating your lease option, ask for as much money in the form of rent credit as you possibly can. As an extreme example, the last lease option deal I did, I got 300 percent of my lease payment to credit toward the purchase price. My deal involved a high-end condominium in South Beach, Florida, with an asking rent of $3,000 a month. Here's the contract I worked out: For the first year, every month that I pay the rent on time, I get three times that—$9,000 each month—as credit toward my down payment for the purchase of the condominium. So over 12 months, that $9,000 will add up to $108,000.

Why would a seller agree to do that? Well, these sellers bought the condo brand new for $450,000 four years ago and it's doubled in value. Today it's worth $1.2 million. They don't really care that they're going to give over $100,000 in credit toward the sales price because they're making a fortune in profit. They got an incredible deal.

You won't usually get 300 percent credit on your lease options, but why did it happen this time? Because I asked for it. You should at least get 5 percent to 10 percent of your lease payment, 20 percent to 30 percent if you can, going toward the purchase price. Be sure to ask.

Repairs

The repair clause on your lease will stipulate that you, the buyer, will be responsible for the first $300 or $500 of repairs. You've sold the landlord on helping him get out of the repair business. This is how you do it. But you don't want to get stuck with doing the repairs yourself. When you turn around and lease option or rent-to-own to other people, they're going to be responsible for the repairs. You'll write that into their lease. Make sure to preapprove and prequalify them; never skip that step.

Down Payment

The sellers will ask for a down payment when you take over the property. Negotiate as low an option down payment as possible. Point out that the property needs repairs and you'd rather spend the extra money on repairs. They may request one or two months rent as option money. Try to negotiate your way out of it. If they refuse, make a business decision about whether to complete the deal.

Protecting Yourself

In your considerations, take into account that you've got to make sure you can rerent the property you lease option. Protect yourself by running an ad, calling on similar For Rent ads, and talking to market professionals to see what the market value actually is.

Another way to reduce your risk in a lease option is to give yourself a 30-day contingency stated like this: "This lease option is contingent on my taking over the property and trying to put it on my program for 30 days." Then advertise it or talk to the real estate agents and managers to see if you can rent it. If no one calls you in 30 days, either exercise your contingency or renegotiate.

Remember to disclose everything you do in writing. Disclose to the original seller that you may rerent it, sublet it, or resell it.

How would you like to have had every property in your town lease optioned 10 years ago at the rents and prices 10 years ago, and have an 11-year lease option? What's going to happen to property in your town in the next 5, 10, or 15 years? In the real market, I have lease options at various terms: for 1 year, 2 years, 3, 5, 10, and so on. Simply go out there and do the best you can.

It's a numbers game that takes calling on a lot of For Rent ads and talking to a lot of landlords. Someday, you may even hit the bonanza and find a landlord who has more than one property that he's tired of managing. You might be able to lease option a lot of them at once.

DAY 34 Action Plan

It's Up to You to Make It Happen!

✔ Again, call on 10 For Rent ads, 10 more For Rent ads, 10 more For Rent ads—up to 50 For Rent ads using your two hours, until you reach a few people.

✔ Make those phone calls to those who didn't call you back from your list of people you called over the last few days. Remember, a policy and procedure I use effectively is to call people every day until you get a response.

✔ Your goal is to get a signed lease, with a signed option. Then record that option.

Contact _____ Property _____

Response _____

_____

Contact _____ Property _____

Response _____

_____

Contact _____ Property _____

Response _____

_____

Contact _____ Property _____

Response _____

_____

Contact _____ Property _____

Response _____

_____

Contact _____ Property _____

Response _____

_____

Contact _____ Property _____

Response _____

_____

Contact _____ Property _____

Response _____

_____

Contact _____ Property _____

Response _____

_____

Contact _____ Property _____

Response _____

_____

Lease Optioning, Part 5

There is another side of lease optioning—when you turn around and find lease optioners after you've found the property.

Preparing to Lease Option to Renters

Your considerations include:

- Option money
- Repairs
- Preapproval
- Length of lease
- Disclosures

Option Money

How much option money or down payment money should you collect when you're lease optioning a property or selling it on owner's terms? As much as possible. Consider this: If someone doesn't have any money to put down, he or she probably won't be a good renter.

Generally, you want at least two or three months of rental payment up front as option money. If the lease optioners don't have an extra two or three months cash, they'll probably fail to pay their rent on time. This means that if they get in trouble, you'll have a problem.

If you've set rent at $1,000 a month, you'll want to collect $3,000. Of course, you never tell them that. You've learned from negotiating techniques (see Days 16 and 17) never to mention a number first. Instead, ask how much money they have to put down. You know that you'd like to have $3,000 up front. But what if they say they've got $8,000. Then you say, "We might be able to work something out."

You may be amazed whom you can attract to your lease option property. A lot of people who are self-employed don't think they have good credit, but they have a lot of cash. Some of them are willing to put a lot of money down because they want to park it somewhere. You solve their problem by lease optioning the property to them for one year. After one year, if they don't buy it, they lose their option money. They also lose their option money if they don't pay the rent on time every month.

The option money goes into your pocket. It's yours. They paid you for the right to buy the property. However, if they *do* buy the property, you may need access to that cash to go toward the purchase price or the down payment. But it's your money; you don't pay taxes on it until the option to buy is exercised or they walk away from the option. I recommend you hold it and be prepared for any of these outcomes. I always like it best when people buy the property; you make the real money when you sell it.

Repairs

The lease optioners are responsible for doing small repairs on the property. Be sure to inspect it to make sure they're doing those repairs under $500 or $1,000, because sometimes they neglect this responsibility. If they don't do the repairs, they lose their option money.

Preapproval

I like to encourage homeownership, so I strive to sell the lease optioners the property. I send them to an affiliated mortgage broker to get them preapproved. While most lease optioners don't think they can qualify for a loan, many can. There are many great loan programs available today. Once they have been preapproved, they can buy the property, which is what you want. Then, you can cash out and move on to the next deal.

Always get your buyers preapproved, even if they don't think they can buy. That's also a great way to check their credit.

Length of Lease

When I'm taking over a property, I want to control it for as long as possible. When I'm selling or lease optioning the property to someone else, I want to give that person as short a period as possible. I usually suggest one year, although it's even better to have only six months.

Then, after one year, I have the right to renew the option, have them move, or let them buy the property. Then, I set up a second year. After the second year, I have the same rights. However, I don't think it's wise to lease option my property to someone for *five* years. Why would I do that if I don't have to?

If a great negotiator wanted to lease option a property for three years or more, I'd say, "Great. But I'm going to put in automatic rent increases and have the property go to the full market value of an appraisal, and you've got to give me more option money every year." I suggest getting whatever you can negotiate for. Again, don't give things away that you don't have to. And if you're going to give them extras, make sure you get paid for them in some way.

Disclosures

Remember to disclose everything you do in writing. For example, if you're not sure you have a clear title to the property, disclose that to your lease optioner.

Convert Rental Property to Lease Options

Lease options are also a great way to take over rental property. Whenever I take over a rental property, I go to the tenants with my mortgage broker, show them the benefits of buying a property, and tell them how they could get preapproved. In fact, we can usually process a preapproval right there and then. Often, they can buy the property for less than what they're paying in rent, taking the tax deductions into consideration. They become homeowners and begin to build wealth. A lot of times when I put rental property under contract, I sell it or lease option it immediately to the renters. It's a win-win situation.

DAY 35   Action Plan

It's Up to You to Make It Happen!

✔ Call on 10 For Rent ads, 10 more For Rent ads, 10 more For Rent ads—up to 50 For Rent ads using your two hours, until you get a hold of a few people.

✔ Call those who didn't call you back from your list of people you called over the last few days. Call people every day until you get a response.

✔ Your goal is to get a signed lease, with a signed option. Then record that option.

Contact _____ Property _____

Response _____

_____

Contact _____ Property _____

Response _____

_____

Contact _____ Property _____

Response _____

_____

Lease Optioning, Part 5

Contact _____ Property _____

Response _____

_____

Contact _____ Property _____

Response _____

_____

Contact _____ Property _____

Response _____

_____

Contact _____ Property _____

Response _____

_____

Contact _____ Property _____

Response _____

_____

Contact _____ Property _____

Response _____

_____

Contact _____ Property _____

Response _____

_____

Lease Optioning, Part 6

This is the sixth and final day you'll spend learning about lease optioning in this 40-Day Plan. It's time to put together all you've learned and see how even a not-so-good deal can become a great one.

A Deal in the Making

Let's say you've leased optioned a property for $1,500 a month. It's worth $250,000, and your option is to buy it for $230,000. So you're only going to make $20,000 on this option deal, which is not a very good deal.

Instead, you turn around and lease option the property to a couple for $1,900 a month and send them to one of your affiliated mortgage companies. The company representative tells you they can buy the property right now; the couple is preapproved for $260,000. So you sell them the property for $260,000, recognizing the ever-present 5 percent to 10 percent fudge factor in appraisals. (Of course,

Never rent or lease option a property without first running a credit and criminal background check on everyone that's going to live in it. (When the applicants sign the application, they agree to this credit and criminal background check.) Also, check with at least two previous landlords. In fact, I recommend talking with three previous landlords or hire tenant-screening services to do that for you. Get the tenants to pay for this service through their application fee. Make sure that you screen, screen, screen, and get plenty of references. It's better to have a place empty for six months than have one bad tenant.

it's got to be a reasonable fudge factor because the property must actually be appraised for $260,000.)

Once you have a buyer, you're ready to pay off the original sellers. You had a three-year lease option. Remember that you always ask for a discount, so you go back to the original sellers and say, "I had three years to pay off this money (always count it out, 2005, 2006, 2007)—so it would be August of 2007. If I get that cold, hard cash in your hands a little sooner, what would you do for me?"

You've already asked what they're going to do with the cash when you originally talked to them. Refer back to that knowledge. Ask them if having that cash in hand would help them take a vacation, pay for their retirement, move out of state, go fishing—whatever they like to do. Would that be worth something to them? They'll usually say yes.

Then ask, "What's the least you'd take right now to cash out of this property and be okay?" You don't have to divulge that you're ready to close right now. The seller might say, "Well, under our contract I was going to get $230,000, but I'll take $225,000." Then go right into your negotiating, asking if they can do a little better, what's the least they could take. By the time you stop negotiating, they've agreed to take $220,000.

Next you go to closing. The end buyers pay $260,000, and you pay the original seller $220,000. You've just made $40,000, an extra $20,000. You doubled your profit just by asking for a discount.

DAY 36   Action Plan

It's Up to You to Make It Happen!

✔ Call on 10 For Rent ads, 10 more For Rent ads, 10 more For Rent ads—up to 50 For Rent ads using your two hours, until you reach a few people.

✔ Call those who didn't call you back from your list of people you called over the last few days. Call people every day until you get a response.

✔ Your goal is to get a signed lease, with a signed option. Then record that option.

Contact _____ Property _____

Response _____

_____

Contact _____ Property _____

Response _____

_____

Contact _____ Property _____

Response _____

_____

Contact _____ Property _____

Response _____

_____

Contact _____ Property _____

Response _____

_____

Contact _____ Property _____

Response _____

_____

Contact _____ Property _____

Response _____

_____

Contact _____ Property _____

Response _____

_____

Contact _____ Property _____

Response _____

_____

Contact _____ Property _____

Response _____

_____

✔ Make a lease option plan.

How many properties would you like to lease option in the next six months? _____ In the next year? _____

What type of property—for example, a vacation home, renting it out when you're not there and using it when you'd like to?

_____

_____

What type of cash flow would you like to have from your lease options?

_____

How many of them would you like to close on in a year?

_____

How are you going to find them?

_____

_____

_____

Track your calls and responses. Make sure that you get plenty of market information so you get a good deal.

Buying and Holding Property

Some people want to buy property, hold onto it for a long time, and rent it out. It's a great way to build wealth because if you've bought property for the long term, you have tenants who are paying off your debt.

The beginning process is much the same as you've already learned. You've got to start with a motivated seller. You've already learned how to find motivated sellers through For Rent ads, eviction court, investment property for sale, and real estate agents. You can apply these avenues to finding property to hold.

The next step involves purchasing the property. There are two ways:

1. Use your own money. You can, but I don't recommend it.

2. Use other people's money, owner's terms, or creative finance to buy rental property.

With your partners, hard moneylenders, and knowledge of wholesaling, you now have the ability to take over people's property and quickly make money. Or you can own it and manage it, building long-term wealth.

Property Management

The most critical part of having rental property is management. I highly recommend that you not manage your own property. It's a high liability endeavor. Instead, pay someone from 7 percent to 10 percent to manage your property. You'll need systems in place to screen tenants and collect rent. Set up a business plan detailing how you will manage rental property.

Don't confuse property ownership and property management. No one will manage your property as well as you. I recommend that you implement my landlording systems, policies and procedures, put them in place, and manage the manager. Because if you're managing your property, you'll be stuck answering phone calls, doing repairs, and collecting rent. This will take up much of your time—time you could use calling more For Rent ads, finding more deals.

Consider this: What if you were able to buy one more house each year with the time you used managing property? You have to think about the cost of your time. I think owning rental property long term is a great wealth builder. You just need to reserve your time for doing the activities that make you money.

Finding Rental Property

In addition to all the ways you've already learned to find motivated sellers, when looking for property to buy and hold, try these additional strategies:

- Call another 10 For Rent ads, looking for people who might let you take over their rental property.

- Talk to three real estate agents. Tell them you're looking for investment property that will generate cash flow and that you can buy at a discount.

- Call three other investors you've met through the real estate association. Tell them that you're looking for rental property.

- Run ads saying, "Attention landlords and property managers: Get out of the headache business, call me, I'll take over your rental property."

- Hand out flyers at your real estate association.

- Put up signs saying, "I buy property."

- Every time you talk to landlords, ask them if they know anybody else who has property they might want to sell. Landlords know other landlords.

- Visit your local apartment association. Sometimes, there are small property owners there who own houses, duplexes, and small apartment buildings. Meet them, and announce that you're interested in buying property.

- And as always, track your activities: How many phone calls did you make? Whom did you talk to? What was the response?

Holding or Wholesaling?

Should you invest for the long term, or is wholesaling the best way to generate cash?

Rental property, which is long-term investing, is a great wealth builder. I highly recommend it at some point. But you're never going to make as much money as you think with rental property. By the time the rent comes in, and you pay your mortgage, taxes, insurance, and repairs, and you adjust for vacancy—you might make some cash, but not much.

There are only two times you make money in real estate: when you sell property for profit or when you refinance it and pull some of your equity out in the form of borrowed funds. The best way to generate cash in the beginning is through wholesaling; lease optioning; and buying, fixing, and selling.

I recommend that most people start out wholesaling and lease optioning. Then, when they generate enough cash, and have a big cash cushion, that's the time to get into rental property. Most people do it backwards. They get into rental property, and they get bogged down with cash flow problems. But if you have six months or one year of mortgage payments in the bank, after you've made and saved money wholesaling and lease optioning a bunch of property, the down sides of rental property are not as big an issue because you have a big cash cushion.

DAY 37   Action Plan

It's Up to You to Make It Happen!

✔ On this day, make your buy and hold plan.

What type of rental property would you like?

_____

How much rental property?

_____

How much cash flow would you need a month to keep them running?

_____

How many properties would you like to have this year? _____

Next year? _____ In 3 years? _____ In 4 years? _____

In 5 years? _____ In 10 years? _____

What price range will you look in?

_____

If you're buying property, what kind of net worth do you think you could have, knowing that the tenants will pay off the property?

_____

How are you going to find properties?

_____

_____

_____

_____

_____

_____

How will you finance them?

_____

_____

_____

_____

_____

Property Managers

Put property managers on your team. They're a great source of information concerning market rents and market conditions, such as how quickly things rent. They're also excellent resources for good contractors, repair people, attorneys, title companies, and real estate agents. And, of course, they are excellent sources of deals. Interview them; see if they qualify to manage your property down the road.

The most deals I've ever gotten from a single source were from a property manager in my town. He managed more than 400 properties and let me buy 80 of them. I wholesaled most of them and kept a few.

Contact five property managers and keep track of the response rate.

DAY 38   Action Plan

It's Up to You to Make It Happen!

✔ Contact five property management companies. How can you find them? They advertise in the real estate section of the newspapers, at real estate associations, and at apartment associations. List them here.

_____

_____

_____

_____

_____

✔ Ask property managers if they know people who would like to sell their property. Make it very clear that you're willing to still pay their management fees and commissions. You're looking for lease-option potentials and property that you can buy, fix up, and sell; or buy and hold.

_____

_____

_____

_____

_____

Review Activities

Spend this day, as you should one day every week, reviewing all the activities that you've been doing. That includes all the phone calls you've been making. Make a note about whom you've been talking to and for how long. What results did you get? What have you been doing to make your goals come alive?

Do What You Like Best

Concentrate on activities that you like best—those that you think will make you the most money. As far as the ones you don't like, see if you can eliminate them. Whom can you hire to do them for you? Do an analysis every Friday, and see how much time you're spending on these different activities. What (potentially) is making you the most profit?

Get together with your board of directors. Meet for dinner or lunch, and review all your business practices. Ask these smart business people for their advice—

what should you be doing more of, less of? What suggestions do they have to improve your business?

And always, ask all the people you run into if they know of any property, any buyers, or any people with money. You're always looking for deals and always fine-tuning and streamlining your business.

At this point, if you're having any success or good response, or any problems or questions, please e-mail me using the "Contact Us" button on my web site at www.sheminrealestate.com. Let me know how these success plans are working for you.

The Three Determinants of Success

You've almost worked through the entire 40-Day Plan for Success in real estate investing. Take a moment to review the three determinants of success: desire or belief, knowledge, and persistent action.

Six months from now, if you're not getting what you want from real estate, look at these three things and determine which one is missing. That missing link will hold you back. Forging it will allow you to soar.

Desire or Belief

If you have enough belief or desire that you're going to do real estate investing and succeed, you will succeed. If you don't have enough belief or desire, you won't succeed.

As an example, consider 100 mothers who attended one of my seminars. How many of them would like to follow this 40-Day Plan for Success and learn how to wholesale one property to make an extra $75,000? All the mothers raised their hands. Now, in the real world, only two to five actually wholesaled a property. They learned how to wholesale a property, but they got busy and didn't do it.

Let's say a really bad person kidnapped their children and said, "If you don't wholesale a property in 40 days, then something really bad will happen to them." How many of those 100 mothers would wholesale a property? Each mother would probably wholesale four houses, in 20 days, to keep her children safe.

The only thing that changed was their desire or belief. If you have enough desire, nothing will stop you. If you don't have enough, everything will stop you. So go back to Day 1. What is your desire? Why are you doing this?

Knowledge

Does Bill Gates know everything about computers? No. He hires people who do. The secret of my business is that while I don't know everything, I do know whom to call. If you run into a problem, don't worry or wonder about it, call an expert. That's why you're building your team.

You should have experts in all areas of real estate on your team. You can even call me at 888-302-8018.

Persistent Action

If you keep executing these action plans, even if you don't know what you're doing, something is bound to happen. If you don't do anything, nothing will happen. Persistent action is the area in which most people fail. But you won't, if you follow all 40 days of action plans in this book.

I go to the gym several days a week. When I go at 7:30 A.M., there are about 20 other people working out at that time. Half of that 20 are employees of the gym. This gym has thousands of members, each paying $80 a month. On the most recent January 3 after New Year's Resolutions were made, a couple hundred people showed up at the gym. It was so packed I could hardly get in the door! They had the belief or desire to get in better shape; they also had the knowledge. So why were there only 20 people at the gym a few weeks later? Because the hundreds of resolution makers lacked the third determinant of success: persistent action.

Most people try something new, like quitting smoking or avoiding caffeine, for two or three days. That's not long enough to build up a habit. If you do something consistently and persistently for 40 days, it will become a habit. This works for anything in your life. Make sure you're persistent.

DAY 39 Action Plan

It's Up to You to Make It Happen!

✔ Look back at your Friday reviews and determine:

What activities do you like best?

_____

_____

What comes easiest for you?

_____

_____

What do you like least?

_____

_____

What's hardest for you?

_____

_____

What do you think has the most profit potential for you?

_____

_____

How do you need to adjust your business to take these answers into account?

_____

_____

Growing Your Business

You did it! You reached Day 40. At this point, you should be well along in your investing career. You should be making offers, talking to people, and building your motivated sellers list, buyers list, and money list. I hope you're starting to put properties under contract or at least getting positive responses. Now it's time to think about increasing your business.

Advertising—It Works!

How are you letting people know that you're looking to buy houses, looking for deals, and looking for partners? Do you distribute flyers and cards? Are you running newspaper ads? You need to start budgeting money for advertising.

Invest in Your Education

You're obviously willing to invest in your education because you bought this book. Once you have money coming in, be sure to budget money for your education. Start attending workshops, buying courses, and going to seminars. A good part of your education is talking with other investors over lunch. Just as in any profession, invest in yourself through your continuing education.

Do What Works

It's time to notice what works and to do more of it. If you had success talking to five real estate agents, talk to five more. If you had success calling For Rent ads, call 20 more. If you had success networking at the governmental courts, go back there. If you had success going to your real estate association and networking with other investors, make sure you go back to their meetings.

DAY 40 Action Plan

It's Up to You to Make It Happen!

✔ Make a list of 10 successes that you've had. For example, did you get any positive feedback? Did calling For Rent ads work? Did you find a few people who want to invest with you? Are you getting calls back from letters you sent out or from people you've met?

_____

_____

_____

_____

_____

_____

_____

_____

_____

_____

✔ Make sure you have the reason you're in real estate investing posted in a prominent place on your desk. Review it; rewrite it.

✔ Review all of your business practices.

✔ Go back through the 40-Day Plan for Success. See if you missed anything. What haven't you done? Is there anything you'd like to do again?

_____

_____

_____

_____

_____

You are now armed with simple-to-follow success plans for your real estate investing career. You can succeed if you want to enough. You _will_ do it. Just remember, success is one step at a time, one day at a time. _Happy investing!_

How to Avoid Common Mistakes of New Investors

Heather Seitz

I n August 2001, I read a little book that changed the way I looked at my future and financial goals—and ultimately changed my life.

I read the book in a few hours and knew that it was time to make a change. At the moment I finished reading, I knew I was going to invest in real estate to build my wealth. The only thing I lacked was the knowledge and the confidence to get going. I was afraid to take action. Perhaps you can relate. I have learned (the hard way) that fear can keep people from being successful. Although fear can show up in many ways, it's simply a form of resistance. (If this relates to you, go to www.yamon.net and get the special report titled "7 Critical Success Tips for the NEW Real Estate Investor." Using these tips will help you overcome what's holding you back and will strengthen the characteristics you have for being a good investor.)

Perhaps you're sitting here a year later—or two years or even more than that—after you decided that real estate would be your key to financial freedom. And you still aren't where you want to be. I understand, and it's not your fault!

When I started as an investor, I had been working freelance for about a year following the events of 9/11. Exactly a week before that date, I'd lost my job because the economy was already starting to fail. After 9/11, I refused to "get a job." I was using this as my opportunity to make something different happen in my life. I had earned a living in the corporate world, had experienced what it was like, and knew I didn't want to go back.

I lived month to month, getting in over my head and often not knowing how I'd pay my bills. But I had a dream, my "why." I bought programs off late-night TV, and I circled 50 different ads in the Sunday newspapers with the goal of one day picking up the phone and calling one of the numbers there. Yet anticipating that simple action paralyzed me. I never dialed any of those numbers.

I believe that all things happen in time and that all things happen for a reason. So, in the summer of 2002, I was working at a part-time job teaching computer applications (and I'm not a reformed computer nerd!). It was about 8:30 A.M. on a Tuesday morning when I got a phone call from a friend. Her brother's house was about to go into foreclosure, and he hadn't told anyone until now. Wow . . . was this the opportunity we had been waiting for or what!

Well, as many new investors do, we sat and "thought about it." (I want to emphasize that in this business, you *cannot* "think about it" because if you do, someone else comes along and completes the deal while you're still thinking.) This family home had a $67,000 mortgage and a recent appraisal at $125,000, but it needed a lot of rehab work. Still, it seemed like an investment no-brainer, didn't it?

Well, my friend and I didn't know the first thing about real estate and were absolutely terrified, but we had the presence of mind to recognize a great opportunity. So, as I tend to do, I dove into the deal headfirst. Little did I know that I was on my way to making all the mistakes a new rehabber could possibly make!

In this chapter, I want to share the mistakes I made and note how I got past them by creating systems. Those systems later enabled me to run multiple rehabs simultaneously with a quarter of the time, effort, and resources that I spent on the first one. Instead of spending more than 40 hours a week at my rehabs, I now spend five or six hours a week from start to finish.

Mistake #1: Working Outside of Your Target Market Area

The property we bought was located four hours away from our homes. Once your business is established with duplicative systems in place, it can be easy to expand into additional markets. But in the beginning, stick with your targeted market area. It should be close enough to your home that you can manage the rehab project directly, especially on your first few deals.

A Side Note about Finding Deals Close to Home

1. Choose a target market, a *type of seller* to focus on (foreclosures, absentee owners, divorcees, expired listings, and so forth).

2. Choose a primary communication method (direct mail, driving for dollars, advertising, and so forth). Direct mail is not a target; it is a method of communicating with your target.

3. Choose an exit strategy (wholesale, retail, rental). Again, this is what you are going to do with your deals; it's not a focus.

Take time to figure out what your tolerance is and how involved you need to be in the rehab project. The deal might not have to be in your backyard (though probably plenty exist), but having it four hours away will cost you a lot more time and money.

How to Avoid Mistake #1

The solution is simple: Target a specific area close by, and work it in depth. Sure, you might think your market is saturated and that there are no deals left. But here's a secret. People always say that about *their own market*! The grass is always greener on the other side. In my market, I'm currently rehabbing a deal that has $150,000 in equity. I'm getting ready to close three more rehabs, each with between $20,000 and $40,000 after-repair profits. Thank goodness my market is saturated with other investors!

Don't get caught up looking for greener pastures somewhere else. You will be surprised what's available in your own backyard. If you're looking elsewhere, you're likely just procrastinating and making excuses.

> You can choose to make money or you can choose to make excuses, but you can't choose both, so stop procrastinating and choose one!

Mistake #2: Assuming Good Maintenance without Doing the Proper Inspections

Because this was the family home of a friend, I just assumed everything would have been well cared for because I knew the owners. Never, ever take good maintenance for granted!

On my first rehab, I didn't even know what to start with. The obvious things stuck out—like the rotted wood siding and the pool that was green with pond scum. But I didn't know to look for or to price the "small" details—things like the plumbing, roof, electric, and so on. I hadn't a clue what to look at or even where to look.

How to Avoid Mistake #2

Get familiar with the majors of rehab. These are the items that can cost you big dollars on a deal, things that will make or break a deal, and things that can take you right out of the real estate game. You certainly don't want to become a motivated seller yourself because you got into a bad deal.

The majors of rehab fall into these five categories:

1. Roof
2. Structure (foundation)
3. Electrical
4. Plumbing
5. HVAC (heating, ventilation, and air conditioner)

These might seem scary, but in reality, a little education goes a long way. And the best type of education is hands on. I started by taking bus trips with experts who had experience in these areas. I asked questions and got involved. I also worked closely with my home inspector as I took on more and more rehabs in the beginning of my career.

After I negotiated the contract, I always ordered a professional inspection. This has actually earned me thousands and thousands of dollars in my career. After simply having a third-party expert do the inspection, I found it's almost always possible to renegotiate the price of the contract and receive credit for repairs. (For tips on how to do your own initial inspections, visit www.fixing andflipping.com.)

Mistake #3: Negotiating the Contract

Because the seller of my first rehab was a family member of a friend, it didn't even occur to me to negotiate the deal. We just agreed to everything the seller needed—or should I say *wanted*! We gave him his asking price and let him drive the deal.

This saga gets even better. *We even let him and his family live in the home for the next two months while we rehabbed it and lived in it with him.* Yes, you read that correctly. We moved into the house together with the sellers who were in foreclosure.

How to Avoid Mistake #3

At a minimum, consider these four things when negotiating your contracts:

1. *Price.* Remember to ask, "Is that the best you can do?" Never give sellers what they ask in the first negotiation.
2. *Deposits.* Always give the deposits to a third party or escrow company. Never give funds directly to the seller.
3. *Closing.* When is the closing? Set a firm date.
4. *Occupancy.* Live by the rule called "cash for keys." That means *never, ever* give sellers a single penny until they have left the house and you have taken over occupancy.

Mistake #4: Moving into Your Rehab

As I mentioned, we were living four hours away from the rehab, so we didn't have too much choice about living there in this case. Yet, I constantly hear about students and other investors who plan to move into their rehabs to save money. If you are thinking of doing that, you're going to spend more time and get more frustrated doing the deal. You're also more likely to "overimprove" (put in items that aren't necessary for an investor's purposes) if you're living in the space.

How to Avoid Mistake #4

This one's easy—just don't do it under any circumstance! It will hold up the rehab and cause unnecessary stress. I guarantee. Currently, one of my real estate students is living in the home he's rehabbing. He swears that he's never been so frustrated and so stressed, and he's really angry about how long the rehab is taking.

Mistake #5: Overimproving Your Rehab Property

I expect that you have read a book, or will in the future, that tells you exactly what each improvement will do for your return on investment. Unfortunately, I took this information too literally. If it said, "You will increase the value by $1000 by adding X fixture," then I bought that fixture. I did this all through our first rehab house. So at the end of the whole project, we believed our house was worth $168,000 but the neighborhood didn't agree. None of the other houses (even the ones in better condition) were selling for more than $130,000 to $150,000. I'm sure you know what I'm referring to! Realize that sometimes the advice in the books is wrong. Authors often forget to leave out the part that says, "No matter what you do to a property, a neighborhood still has its limitations on the value of upgrades."

How to Avoid Mistake #5

Learn to find accurate comparable sales. You'll always hear someone tell you that her house is "the nicest one on the street" or "has all the upgrades that the others don't." This simply means that the house has been improved too much for the neighborhood. If you're going to make that home your own, then go ahead and improve it in a first-class way. But if you want to turn around and resell it, remember to improve it to the level of neighborhood standards.

Always use your best judgment. That means if you have the option of buying a $20 faucet rather than a $129 faucet, as long as the neighborhood supports it, go for the $20. If you're doing a million-dollar rehab, go for the upgrades. It would be wise to go into other houses for sale in the neighborhood so that you can see the standards your house is competing against.

Mistake #6: Using All of Your Own Money to Fund the Deal

New investors who have money have more of a chance to get into trouble than those without cash or credit.

I had a little cash saved up in my bank account and proceeded to spend it all on rehab and holding costs, which put me in a dire financial position just a few months later. I had violated the one rule that I live by religiously today—*never use your own money*!

How to Avoid Mistake #6

If the deal is good, then you don't *have* to use your own money. People get so caught up on funding and financing, but in reality, if the deal is good, the money will come. You can use a credit partner, a financial partner, or even credit cards or equity lines.

My first rehab was the first and last deal I funded with my own money. From then on, I found people who had money that wasn't bringing in a good return. Usually, I'd offer them 10 percent backed by a note or, better yet, a second mortgage on a property.

After struggling with a partner for a year because we had not tied a loan to real estate and simply gave the investor a promissory note, I was burdened with paying back $30,000 to the investor. So, even if the money is available, still protect yourself with the proper security instruments.

Mistake #7: Not Having Joint Venture Agreements in Place with Partners

I remember reading a book in which the author talked about partnerships and recommended against them. Shortly thereafter, a mentor, coach, and friend warned me against partnerships. However, I thought my circumstances were different and that I could handle my partnership in my first rehab project. I was so wrong! In a short time, my partner and I were at each other's throats. Our first rehab experience ruined both our business and our friendship.

How to Avoid Mistake #7

What I learned later was that partnerships by nature rarely work. The better your friendship or relationship is, the worse it will turn out in the end. Instead, look at the alternative of building many joint ventures. This enables you to do projects on a deal-by-deal basis. You do a deal, if it works out, you do another and another and so on. That way, you're not bound by a partnership, and you're not obligated to each other's personal finances. When you outgrow the relationship, you simply move on to new joint ventures.

Realize that there will never be true equality in a business partnership, so protect yourself and your would-be partner by setting up joint ventures instead. It will save business relationships and friendships. (To download a sample joint venture agreement, visit www.yamon.net)

Mistake #8: Not Having Contractors' Agreements in Place

Many people will tell horror stories about contractors. I also have mine from the first (and second, and even third) time around. But after a few bad experiences, I wised up quite a bit!

On my first deal, the contractors didn't show up on time, did poor work, and refused to finish the job. In fact, at the end of this job, their licenses were taken away by the state. On my second deal, I paid the contractor too much up front before the job was complete. The workers never finished the job and became sloppy with the labor they did do.

How to Avoid Mistake #8

Put a simple contractor's agreement in place. By getting a good agreement and having a local attorney review the contract, you can protect yourself from disagreements over important issues.

Always ask your contractors to bid the job in terms of labor, materials, and time, and make your selection according to each of those factors. Then, include a penalty if they take longer on the job than the agreed-upon date. Countless people have told me that contractors don't go for this. This is simply not true. *The key is that you absolutely* must *have your contractor include a time frame in the estimate.* If the contractor tells you the project will take three weeks and the crew has to work beyond four weeks, then it's absolutely acceptable that you start penalizing them in an amount equal to your daily holding costs. If the contractor tries to argue, simply say, "But, Mr. Contractor, you told me it would take only three weeks, and I'm giving you four. Are you saying that your bid was not truthful?"

In practice, I usually give the contractor one week leeway because of unforeseen circumstances, and I also always include a clause in which environmental delays are excluded from the contract. For example, in South Florida during the rainy season, you can't penalize someone if it takes an extra week to paint a house because it's raining. Weather factors are simply out of anyone's control. (To find out how to get your own Contractor Agreement and have an attorney review it for you for less than $30, visit www.organizedrehab.com.)

Mistake #9: Not Building a Buyers List

When the rehabbing is complete, it's simply too late to start marketing. I used to finish my rehabs before I even posted the For Sale sign in the front yard and found out how much time I lost unnecessarily.

How to Avoid Mistake #9

The moment you leave the closing table, head straight to your building supply store and purchase a "For Sale By Owner" sign. Then immediately post it in the front yard. You are probably saying to yourself, "Surely I can't let anyone into the house in this condition." And you are correct. You absolutely cannot and should not let someone into a house that is only partially rehabbed. I seem to be contradicting myself. However, all you need to do is politely explain that because of insurance purposes, you can't let anyone in the house until the repairs are done, but you would be happy to add them to your buyers list. You'll call as soon as the rehabilitation on the home is finished.

This policy serves you in several ways. First, it creates a list of interested people you can bring through the home the day you are ready to show it. Second, it gives you the opportunity to get information about the kinds of buyers who are interested in the home. Third, it provides an opportunity to take customers who don't have an interest in buying this home and turn them toward other properties you may have. You're looking to make money from another deal.

There are many other benefits to building a buyers list. Just remember, it's important to begin to market on the day you close on the property. Many rehabbers forget to calculate the time it takes to sell a house, so reduce your costs by starting to market it immediately after you buy it.

Mistake #10: Not Getting the Right Insurance

You probably already know that, before you close on a deal, you must purchase insurance on the property. Well, it's not quite that easy. A normal homeowner's policy won't cover you when the property is vacant or when a rehab is going on, because a lot more risks are involved in insuring a property that's vacant, especially one that has workers coming in and out.

How to Avoid Mistake #10

Find some kind of builder's risk policy. Usually, these policies will be available through your local agents, more so than through large insurance companies. You can locate insurers through your local real estate investors clubs. (For a directory of clubs, visit the links section on www.yamon.net.) Make sure their policies cover vacant homes and ones that are being rehabbed. In addition, look for companies that will prorate the premiums or let you pay on them monthly. I currently work with two agents. One will prorate if the property sells in less than a year, and the other will allow me just to make monthly payments based on the annual policy rate.

Also, consider any additional coverages that you might want. For example, if you live in a flood zone, you could be required to carry flood insurance. Or, during certain seasons, like hurricane season for example, you could be required to carry wind insurance. Some of these requirements may be dictated by the lender and others not. Use your best judgment.

Mistake #11: Closing into Your Own Name, Not a Company Name

At some point in most all investors' careers, they inevitably close a home into their own name, perhaps because of financing or because of lack of knowledge.

How to Avoid Mistake #11

If you have a property in your name, you must put together a business entity and deed the property into the entity. It's that simple. Just set up a business entity (Corporation or Limited Liability Company), and move the property into that entity. This will help shield you from liability and keep people from trying to sue you.

Even if you close the property into an entity, it's also a good idea to have some kind of legal protection. I got involved with Pre-Paid Legal Services in order to protect me from lawsuits, to have someone read over contracts, and so forth. (For information on this service, visit www.yamon.net.)

Mistake #12: Using Cheap Supplies

Keep in mind, I didn't say "inexpensive" supplies; I said cheap! If you can get good quality supplies for inexpensive prices, then go for it. However, I'm talking about going into a discount store and getting the cheapest five-gallon container of paint you can find. You may be laughing now, but I assure you that if you do this, you will live to regret it.

On my first rehab deal, that's precisely what I did. I went in and bought two five-gallon containers of paint and cheap primer. Well, the job took two five-gallon containers of primer and a total of four five-gallon containers of paint. Add in the time factor, and you can see how this was *not* a money-saving maneuver.

How to Avoid Mistake #12

Although it certainly is enticing to spend less money on supplies than you have to, it can cost you more in time and labor down the line. If you're on a tight budget, you might consider creative alternatives like getting several gallons of "oops" paint mixed by mistake from your home supply store at around $5 a gallon. These are usually pretty good quality brands. Then, buy a 25-gallon garbage pail and mix them all together. You will have better quality paint at the same, if not a lower, price than the "bargain" paint.

For other things, seek out local stores where you can get supplies at a discount. For example, in many cities, there are Habitat for Humanity stores where you can pick up materials at reduced prices. There are often wholesalers of cabinetry, carpet, tile, and so on where you can get discounts to help defray some of the costs.

At the end of the day, you'll want to weigh the pros and the cons of time, labor, and materials. (Sound familiar? See Contractor Agreements.)

Mistake #13: Not Planning an Exit Strategy

Let's suppose you have rehabbed a house. It looks great, it's in a good neighborhood, but it's just not selling. What do you do? Panic? Stress? Become a motivated seller yourself? I have been here, too! I have done my repairs and for one reason or another not been able to move the house within my 90-day window. (Adjust that number for your marketplace.) Well, panicking and stressing will do you no good. You need to look at other options.

My first deal sat vacant, sucking holding costs out of me month after month for nearly six months. I didn't know what to do and didn't know how to get out of it. I didn't have an exit strategy. I was ready to let it go just to recoup my costs. Part of the problem was simply timing; I had it on the market over the holiday season.

How to Avoid Mistake #13

Every property has its unique challenges, but by learning what methods are out there to move properties and using creative financing techniques to your benefit, you'll be ahead of the curve.

When I first found myself without an exit strategy, I ended up taking a three-day training course. At this course, I listened in on a section about creative finance. The instructor offered strategy after strategy, although some of them went right over my head and others just confused me. But several of them made sense, and I saw how I could implement them on the deal I wasn't able to move otherwise.

From that time on, I realized that flexibility is one of the most important characteristics of an investor. If something isn't working, be prepared to try something else. I realized that I had to think outside of the box and look beyond the option of just selling the property outright. By doing so, I had the property under contract for more than the asking price within three days.

Always, always have another alternative or two at your disposal. In rehabs, in many cases, you simply want to flip the property and cash out of the deal. But, in some cases, that may not be the best strategy, so look at your alternatives. Always be open to the idea of refinancing and then renting or lease optioning or seller financing if the underlying financing allows. The key here is to be creative and not to limit your thinking about the possibilities. When you go into a deal, always have at least two to three ways out.

Mistake #14: Underestimating Holding Time

This becomes more and more challenging the better you get in this business, believe it or not, because you tend to think that you can move things faster. However, it can also be a challenging estimate to come up with in the beginning as well—even scary. I always used to think I could turn a property in 45 to 60 days. The reality was that usually I could do so in about 90 days. There was always that one deal that just wouldn't sell fast enough.

How to Avoid Mistake #14

First of all, do your due diligence. You need to see how long properties are typically staying on the market in a certain area. Median-priced homes will typically move the fastest because the majority of people are looking in this price range. Higher-priced homes will often sit on the market longer, waiting for that special buyer. And with lower-priced homes it may be harder to get your buyers qualified. These variations, of course, will also vary from market to market, but they are a general rule of thumb.

After you have an idea as to how long your home will be on the market, you will better be able to estimate this figure. You also must realistically estimate the time for repairs (see Mistake #8). If the contractor goes over budget, you should be covered on the holding costs. But it's important to take into account the time for repairs. If it's going to take 90 days for repairs, you obviously cannot turn the home over in 90 days.

And lastly, you should be building your buyers list right away. This way, when the repairs are done, you will minimize your holding time and increase your profit potential (see Mistake #9).

Mistake #15: Underestimate Holding Costs

It's easy to get caught up in the excitement of doing a deal, and it's inevitable that you will leave out some of the costs unintentionally. Unfortunately, depending on the situation, such mistakes can cost you several hundred dollars a month and thousands of dollars over the project. Perhaps you didn't think about all the utilities, for example. Perhaps you are in a county or city that has different types of fees and taxes. Perhaps certain things are or are not included in various bills.

How to Avoid Mistake #15

The holding costs you must account for and take into consideration are electric, water, waste, insurance, taxes (even if they aren't due monthly, they are still a cost that will reduce your profits), lawn service, snow removal, pool service, homeowners' association (HOA) fees or maintenance fees, and so on. In some cities and counties, waste removal will be included with water. In others, it won't be.

   If your property is part of an HOA or in a condo building, there will also be fees associated with the property. You need to know what those fees cover and what you'll be responsible for individually. These little things add up and will start to cost you lots of money each month.

Mistake #16: Not Tracking Expenses Appropriately

It's easy to get behind on accounting for your properties. Receipts get lost. Things get misplaced. You can't remember if you bought this ceiling fan for one property or the other. If you are in the deal with a joint venture partner, then sloppiness can get especially messy and even hurt your relationship. At the end of the deal, you have no idea exactly what you made on it.

How to Avoid Mistake #16

You need to come up with some kind of tracking system that lets you enter all the receipts *plus* keep copies of all receipts. You can simply tape them to a blank sheet of paper and put them in a three-ring binder.

So you think this effort is overkill? Let me explain the reasons for doing it a little differently!

When you turn around and sell your property in 83 days, the lender for your buyer is going to give you a friendly call in which she will politely ask you why you are making such a big profit on a $200,000 deal. In the meantime, you have been rehabbing the property and think that the profit is not nearly enough. Let's say you bought it for $150,000 and are selling it for $200,000 less than three months later. But the bank sees a $50,000 profit from this deal.

You and I both know that you aren't making anywhere close to $50,000 on the deal. But, in the world of lending, you're guilty until proven innocent!

What about closing costs? Holding costs? Interest Payments? Repairs? The bank's answer to you is "Okay, prove it." If you can't prove it, you're making money in their eyes and the deal might not go through. The bank's goal is to protect the buyer's interests, and there's nothing you can do about it except overcome the bank's false impression before it becomes an obstacle.

By gathering all of the receipts and an itemized spreadsheet of all costs, you can simply take them out of your folder or binder and fax them upon request to the lender. This should, in a matter of moments, make the issue go away. If the documentation is already in one place, it won't cost you three to four days of holding costs to gather all the documentation, during which time the buyer might get scared and back out!

If that's not a good enough reason, I have three more words for you: Capital Gains Tax. If you can prove that you incurred the expenses, you're not taxed on them! (To find information on budget tracking and organizing the rehab project, visit www.organizedrehab.com and www.fixingandflipping.com.)

Action Plan

Now that you know some of the biggest mistakes new investors make on their deals, let's create a specific action plan to get through your first rehab. Follow these 16 steps.

1. Find the Deal

All real estate begins with the deal. If you don't have a deal, then walk away. As I mentioned earlier, I recommend that you target a specific type of seller and work from there. There are many profit centers within each type of motivated seller category; if you don't take the time to learn each and every profit center, you could be leaving thousands of dollars on the table. How do you find the deal?

- Choose a type of seller to target (preforeclosure, evictions, expired listings, etc.).

- Choose a method of communication (direct mail, advertising, telephone, driving for dollars).

- Choose an exit strategy (wholesale, rehab or rent). If the deal doesn't fit your goals, network with another investor whose strategy it does fit.

Once you have found the deal, track it so you know where the majority of your deals are coming from. People spend so much money in real estate, often not having a clue as to where the profits are going.

If you get 50 percent of your deals from the multiple listing service (MLS), but you spend 75 percent of your time and resources mailing to people on a pre-foreclosure list, you might want to reconsider your strategy.

For more information on finding deals and getting started, visit www.thecompleteguidetogettingstarted.com.

2. Do an Initial Inspection

This is when you do your own walk through. You are looking for any major problems and beginning to build your budget. You will want to take some tools with you such as the following:

- ❏ Measuring tape, to measure all room dimensions and windows and doors
- ❏ Slab of marble, to see if the floors are level (if the marble shoots off in one direction, you may have a foundation problem)
- ❏ Screwdriver, to check any soft/damp spots
- ❏ Camera, to take initial photos that you'll refer to later on

For a complete list, visit www.fixingandflipping.com.

Remember, this is only your initial inspection to help you structure your offer. This number can, and often does, change once you have your professional inspection. You can always renegotiate later. Action is the first step! We are conditioned to think about things throughout our lives. I encourage you to act first and then finish thinking about the deal later.

3. Submit Your Offer or Contract

Now that you have found the deal and completed your basic walkthrough, you want to submit your offer. Pay special attention to the effective date, closing date, and any key dates and dollar amounts that are a part of the deal.

Remember, the contract is not effective until both parties agree to all terms and sign and date. Always mark the effective date so that you have an accurate record.

When the contract becomes effective, the rehab clock starts ticking. You have anywhere from 30 to 120 days to get this thing closed. This all depends on your negotiating power and the contract that you finally agree to. Nonetheless, the countdown begins, regardless how long or short that timeline might be.

Don't do what most investors do at this point!

Most investors just stop and wait until closing. I assure you that if you do that, you are going to lose a *lot* of money on each deal that you do. If you take the next 30 to 40 days to get this deal moving, you will save *at least* 30 to 40 days of holding time, and time is money, literally.

4. Put Together a Memo

Do this so that you will always be able to know, at any given time, what your dates and deadlines are. You certainly don't want to go into breach of contract because you didn't meet a deadline. Or if you are using your inspection as one of your contingencies out of the contract and miss it by several days, you could forfeit your deposit. (You can find these documents at www.organizedrehab.com.)

5. Set Up a Professional Inspection

You may be sitting there saying, "I know enough about contracting" or "I've already done my own rehabs." That's fine. You probably do have a good idea of everything that needs to be done and an accurate estimate of such repairs. But let's look at it from the sellers' standpoint. You are the buyer, the investor. They are already probably a little bit guarded if you have negotiated down the price since the deal began. You have finally come to an agreement. In their minds, that is your offer. It is very hard for you to come back and renegotiate.

Now is the time to bring out the "professional"—a neutral individual who will give an objective report. I have used the same inspector for every single property that I do in my local farm area. He provides me with a report and estimates of all costs. I take this report back to the sellers and simply open it up, saying, "I just want to show you what came back."

Then, I stay quiet. I don't ask for anything. I don't try and renegotiate. I just show them the report. With only one exception, I have had the seller come back to me and tell me that they are willing to knock out $2,000, $3,000, or more. On one deal, I got $15,000 taken off the contract price simply because I faxed the report over. That one deal paid for my next 50 inspections.

If you are going to use this strategy, then your report *must* have repair estimates on the report. (To view a sample report, visit www.organizedrehab.com.)

6. Prepare Your Budget

You have done your own estimates and brought in the professional inspector. You should have a pretty good idea of what things are going to cost you at this point. I use a software application that is simple to use. I just enter the dimensions of a room, and the software calculates my costs to tile, carpet, paint, etc. I enter the number of fixtures or ceiling fans, and it calculates prices. I put this together because I didn't want to reinvent the wheel. I wanted a system that is easy to use and duplicatable from deal to deal. You can either purchase a prepackaged application or create one yourself. (For a simple budget worksheet, visit www.fixingandflipping.com or www.organizedrehab.com.)

7. Prepare a Property Marketing Plan

You should only be about two to three days into the contract right now. The maximum amount of time invested should be a week, and the only reason to take a week is that you couldn't schedule your inspector right away. Most investors will be tempted to stop at this point, but I encourage you to follow these steps through. Because you're still in the due diligence phase, you have the opportunity to uncover additional things and renegotiate the contract if need be. Initially, I put together a property plan to get a hard-money loan from an investor. My plan was in the form of a 12-page report that I do on every deal. It included a project summary, a summary of the specific market, a budget, a rough timeline, comparable sales, and a plan to market the property. The marketing plan included three separate profit potentials from best-case scenario to probable-case scenario to worst-case scenario. Doing this property marketing plan (PMP) forces you to really analyze the deal and look at where all of your dollars will be spent. It takes about an hour to complete, but gives you a clear picture of the project. That hour will save you time during the rehab and the marketing phases of every project.

To summarize, doing this plan serves three main purposes.

1. First, it makes you closely evaluate the deal by taking out the emotional aspect and looking strictly at factual data.

2. Second, you can use this information to shop out the financing to potential lenders. Most lenders will not require such an extensive report, but it's always better to have and not need than need and not have. You are also showing potential lenders that you are treating this as a business and that you are a professional.

3. Third, when you decide to start getting into multifamily properties or commercial real estate, you'll have something tangible to show that you have treated your business as a business rather than as a weekend hobby.

8. Find Financing

At this point, you're ready to find a lender. Even if you have the cash to do the deal yourself, find a lender who will keep you from getting into bad deals. Much of the time, when you are doing rehabs, you will turn to hard moneylenders who are private lenders with funds available to rehabbers. Depending on your market and the lender, you will pay between 1 and 10 points up front (1 point = 1 percent) and between 10 percent to 18 percent interest on the money. These lenders will typically lend between 60 percent to 75 percent of the ARV (after repair value). If you can find a willing lender, then you're safe to bet you've got yourself a deal with room for profit.

Financing can come in many forms other than hard moneylenders. In the course of your business, you'll run in to private lenders who will lend you money at better rates than hard money, and these relationships usually develop over time. You can also find joint venture partners to go in on deals with you. Many initial deals I did involved hard moneylenders to cover the purchase of the property and joint venture partners to cover the holding costs and the repairs. I would simply put together a document with another individual that would pay for all of the repairs and holding costs. You can pay a percentage or a give a percent ownership in the deal. Don't hesitate to get creative when dealing with joint venture partners.

9. Line Up Contractors

In your contract, include a clause that allows you access to the property with a 24-hour notice. Don't abuse this, but use it wisely to bring in your contractors to give you estimates and bids on the projects that need to be done.

In the beginning, depending on your farm area, call between five and seven contractors for each job so you can get three to show up and find one you want to work with. (For links to find local contractors, visit www.yamon.net in the links section.)

You should be no more than two to three weeks into the contract to line up a contractor, depending on how long you have to close. If you have a 30-day contract, you should have a contractor at about Day 14, for example. Put estimates together quickly, and make your decision prior to the close. Remember, have the contractor bid time, labor, and materials. The "cheapest" might not really cost you the least in the long run. *Look especially closely at time estimates!* By spending a few days lining up contractors, you will be ready to start rehabbing the day you get the keys in your hand. Can you see how this could save you days, even weeks, of paying out holding costs?

10. Put Your Budget on Paper

You are ready to put the budget on paper. You have already done your own estimates, which should come in close to where the contractors are, and you can really detail the budget. You want to know where your money is going because, inevitably, you'll spend more on your rehab than you thought. If you learn to manage the budget well, you'll know when you go over in one area, and if and where you can reduce some costs.

11. Line Up Your Insurance

Don't get to the closing table only to find out you forgot to get insurance. You will hold up the closing, or worse, have an uninsured property. You can find insurance agents that will insure vacant properties by asking local investors for recommendations, searching the Internet, or calling around. Keep in mind that many companies will not insure vacant property.

Line up this insurance about a week before closing. And remember to find out whether you can pay monthly under a master policy or whether they will prorate the policy and credit you back if you close within the next 12 months.

In addition to your insurance policy, get copies of proof of insurance from your contractors. They *must* have their own liability insurance. No discussion; this is not an option.

12. Go to Closing

Once you have completed steps 1 through 11, you are finally ready to go to closing. It is quite a relief to be ready to go and to be organized when you are walking out of closing! If you take these steps, then you will never be stressed or overwhelmed as you leave. Keep in mind, however, that in many deals, something always comes up that's out of your control prior to the closing. So even if you follow each of these steps to a the letter, it's still possible that something comes up on the title or that the seller has a change of heart or any number of other issues that could arise. The key is to remain calm, cool, and collected! I remember coaching one of my students through a close that he was ready to back out of. Realize that you are getting great deals because of your ability to solve problems. Take each issue as a miniproblem and solve it. You will do more deals than your competitors if you learn to find solutions instead of panicking like a deer caught in headlights.

13. Rehab the Property

You have done all the prep work, and the job should be relatively seamless; from this time forward, it is just a matter of managing the property. There are steps and sequences that you can follow, but common sense dictates most of it. You wouldn't think to install carpet before you paint the walls or to landscape before you bring in the dumpster, for example. (For a complete system on managing rehabs from start to finish, visit www.organizedrehab.com and www.fixingandflipping.com.)

14. Document, Document, Document

Take photos at the beginning, during the progress, and at the end of the rehab. Track your numbers, and always know where you are on the project. This will keep you from getting in over your head and will keep the job fun! You will have an ongoing documentary of the deals you are doing, and you can show others the whole story of each property.

15. Evaluate the Deal

This does not mean only looking at the final numbers. You want to know where you stand financially, but you also want to take some time and look at what went well, what didn't go so well, and what was just an absolute disaster. This is the only way that you can make corrections on the next go around.

> *Things that went well.* Repeat them and perfect them.
>
> *Things that didn't go so well.* Correct them and modify them until they work.
>
> *Things that were disastrous.* Do not ever repeat them. Consider them lessons learned!

16. Do Another Deal

In summary, rehabbing can be lots of fun, and it can also be challenging. New things always come up on every job, but many things stay the same. These details can be systematized and delegated to someone else. The entire rehab system that I have developed came from completing deal after deal. I have tweaked the system slightly time and time again until it finally became something that I could turn over to someone else to manage.

When I first met Robert Shemin, I remember sitting in the room and watching him make this all look so simple. I was a novice at the time and was just amazed at how he made it all sound so easy. So, I asked him one day, "How do you do so many deals, speak, teach, write books and home study courses, *and* have a life?" What he said to me has stuck with me ever since that time. He told me several things, but I consider these three the most important:

1. *Set a schedule and stick to it.* If your office hours are 10–6, shut the phone off at 6 P.M. Nothing is so urgent that it can't wait until tomorrow. You will get more done in less time if you set limits.

2. *Put systems together.* If you have a system, you don't have to think about it. What separates successful investors from mediocre investors (or those who are just scraping by) are systems. People with systems can turn them over to employees, partners, and so on, and go on with their lives. People without systems are tied to their businesses for the rest of their lives. Put your systems in place, and

walk away! I'm able to spend my time finding deals, negotiating contracts, and structuring the financing—the important details.

3. *Never let people leave without asking what you can do for them.* Robert didn't actually say this to me, but he demonstrated it when I first met. I never realized the impact of this until I was sitting with some speakers and one gentleman kept asking the other for something for free. After about 10 minutes, the first gentleman turned to him and said, "Maybe you should be more like Heather. She never leaves without asking if there's anything she can do. You'll get a lot more that way!" I remember thinking at that moment just how important this lesson of Robert's was to me. Several years later, I find that to be one of the things I cherish most about Robert, his generosity and his genuine sincerity in helping people!

I urge you to take action, implement systems, and start doing deals. The first step is the hardest, but you can't get to your goals without taking that step. Follow *Shemin's 40 Days to Success* and you will be depositing checks in your bank account in no time.

The web resources referenced in this chapter are:

www.yamon.net (general information including links, resources, etc.)

www.organizedrehab.com (rehab project management system that puts more cash in your pocket even if you've never picked up a hammer before; faster, better, and with less effort.)

www.fixingandflipping.com (learn to inspect properties; find out what to look for, how to determine major repairs versus minor repairs, and in what order you should do your repairs)